Robert Browning

A Study of his Poetry

Robert Browning, May 22nd, 1859
A portrait by Rudolf Lehmann

By courtesy of the Trustees of the British Museum

ROBERT BROWNING

A Study of his Poetry

Thomas Blackburn

The Woburn Press — London

This edition published in 1973 by
WOBURN BOOKS LIMITED
67 Great Russell Street
London WC1B 3BT

First published in 1967

Copyright © Thomas Blackburn 1967

ISBN 0 7130 0083 X

Printed in Great Britain by
Lowe & Brydone (Printers) Ltd., Haverhill, Suffolk

For Margaret

Contents

Acknowledgements

Acknowledgements of sources quoted are given in the footnotes on the page.

In addition the author would like to thank Laurence Pollinger Ltd and the Estate of the late Mrs Frieda Lawrence for the quotation from *Psychoanalysis and the Unconscious* by D. H. Lawrence; Mr M. B. Yeats and Macmillan & Co. Ltd for the various quotations from W. B. Yeats's poems; the Literary Executors of the Dylan Thomas Estate; the Trustees of the Joseph Conrad Estate; and all other authors and publishers concerned for permission to reprint copyright material in his book.

Note on the Browning Editions

Both Tennyson and Browning composed with extreme effort and accuracy. They also revised their earlier work in later years. But in their day literary criticism had not become an industry and it was not possible for a poet to sell the contents of his wastepaper basket. This makes for textual difficulties. Professor de Selincourt could produce his admirable edition of Wordsworth because the poet's work was preserved and in longhand through many of its numerous stages by his devoted wife and equally devoted sister. Once the stuff had got into print both Tennyson and Browning showed a remarkable indifference to the vagaries of their printers. Punctuation has only recently been – to some extent – standardized. Every edition of Browning has its own variety of punctuation.

In the quotations for this book I have, for the most part, followed Simon Nowell-Smith's edition for the Reynard Library of Rupert Hart-Davis (1950), but have also made use of the John Murray collection (two volumes, 1919, reprinted 1951) which reprints the two-volume Smith, Elder edition (1896), and the Oxford edition which though cramped is comprehensive. The best selection of Browning's work, although it leaves out *Holy-Cross Day*, *The Heretic's Tragedy* and *Dîs Aliter Visum*, is that made by Nowell-Smith. I refer readers to this admirable work.

11

Although Browning disliked definitives he still needs an editor who will pick his way through the earliest and latest volumes of his poems and find their most satisfactory statement. He also needs an edition of his work which discards its irrelevancies and displays the very considerable number of his significant poems in a form that pleases the eye and is readable.

Besides the works touched on in my Introduction I would also like to mention Professor Langbaum's study, *The Poetry of Experience* (London, 1957) and William Clyde DeVane's *A Browning Handbook* (New York, 1955). The poet has always been lucky in his excellent handbooks.

A considerable number of critical essays have been written on Browning and his poetry. Some of the best of these have been edited by Philip Drew in *Robert Browning: A Collection of Critical Essays* (Methuen, 1966). The first section of the book 'seeks to represent the extremes of hostile and friendly criticism by those to whom Browning was still a modern poet'. It includes essays by Henry James, George Santayana and Roger Lubbock and is of great interest. The book also includes John Stuart Mill's note on *Pauline* which had considerable influence on the poet's development.

A Chronology of Browning's Life

1812 Born May 7 at Camberwell, son of Robert and Sarah Anne (*née* Wiedemann) Browning.

1814 Birth of Sarianna (sister to the poet) (died April 22, 1903).

1828⎫
1829⎭ At London University.

1833 (March) Publication of *Pauline*.

1834 (Spring) Visited St Petersburg.

1835 (August) Publication of *Paracelsus*.

1837 (May 1) Publication of *Strafford*, produced simultaneously at Covent Garden by Macready.

1838 (April to July) Visited Italy for the first time.

1840 (March) Publication of *Sordello*.

1841 (April) Publication of *Bells and Pomegranates* I, *Pippa Passes*.

1842 (March 12) Publication of *Bells and Pomegranates* II, *King Victor and King Charles*; and (November 26) III, *Dramatic Lyrics*.

1843 (January) Publication of *Bells and Pomegranates* IV, *The Return of the Druses*; and (February 11) V, *A Blot in the 'Scutcheon*, produced at Drury Lane by Macready the same day.

1844 (April 20) Publication of *Bells and Pomegranates* VI, *Colombe's Birthday*, produced at the Haymarket by Phelps, April 25, 1853.

(September to December) Revisited Italy.

1845 (May 20) Met Elizabeth Barrett. (November 6) Publication of *Bells and Pomegranates* VII, *Dramatic Romances and Lyrics*.

1846 (April 13) Publication of *Bells and Pomegranates* VIII, *Luria* and *A Soul's Tragedy*. (September 12) Married

13

Elizabeth Barrett; (September 19) eloped. Lived next fifteen years mainly in Italy.

1849 (January) Publication of *Poems* (2 vols). (March 9) Birth of his son, Robert Wiedemann Barrett (nicknamed 'Pen' or 'Penini'). (March 18) Death of his mother.

1850 (April 1) Publication of *Christmas-Eve and Easter-Day*.

1852 (February) Published introductory essay to *Letters of Percy Bysshe Shelley*.

1855 (November 17) Publication of *Men and Women* (2 vols).

1861 (June 29) Death of Elizabeth Barrett Browning. Thereafter lived mainly in London but often visited Brittany and (after 1878) sometimes Italy.

1862 (December) Publication of *Selections* (Forster and Procter, dated 1863).

1863 (August) Publication of *Poetical Works* (3 vols). A new edition followed in 1865 (March).

1864 (May 28) Publication of *Dramatis Personae*; (September) a new edition.

1865 (October) Publication of *Selections* (by Browning), supplementary to Forster and Procter's edition (see above).

1866 (June 13) Death of Robert Browning, senior, the poet's father. Thereafter Browning and his sister Sarianna lived together.

1867 (June 26) Hon. MA, Oxford; (October) Hon. Fellow of Balliol.

1868 (March to July) Publication of *Poetical Works* (6 vols). (November 21) Publication of *The Ring and the Book*, I; and (December 26) II.

1869 (January 30) Publication of *The Ring and the Book*, III; and (February 27) IV. A new edition followed in 1872.

1871 (August) Publication of *Balaustion's Adventure* (reprints followed in 1872 and 1881). (December) Publication of *Prince Hohenstiel-Schwangau*.

1872 (June) Publication of *Fifine at the Fair*. (December) Publication of *Selections* (afterwards called 'first series'), not identical with the preceding volumes.

1873 (May) Publication of *Red Cotton Night-Cap Country*.

1875 (April 15) Publication of *Aristophanes' Apology*. (November) Publication of *The Inn Album*.

1876 (July 18) Publication of *Pacchiarotto*.

1877 (October 15) Publication of *The Agamemnon of Æschylus*.

1878 (May 15) Publication of *La Saisiaz* and *The Two Poets of Croisic*. The former was inspired by the death of his friend, Anne Egerton-Smith, September 14, 1877.

1879 (April 28) Publication of *Dramatic Idyls*. A new edition, called 'first series', followed in 1882.

1880 (May) Publication of *Selections*, second series. (July) Publication of *Dramatic Idyls*, second series.

1881 Foundation of the Browning Society.

1883 (March) Publication of *Jocoseria*. Reprinted in April and May.

1884 (November 21) Publication of *Ferishtah's Fancies*. Reprinted December, and February, 1885.

1887 (January) Publication of *Parleyings with Certain People of Importance in their Day*.

1888 Publication of *Poetical Works* (16 vols). Vol. XVII,
1889 *Asolando*, was added in 1894.

1889 (December 12) Publication of *Asolando*, dated 1890. The sixth edition was published in January, 1890.

Venice, December 12, died. (December 31) Buried at Poets' Corner, Westminster Abbey.

Introduction

As a schoolboy, I was inoculated against the poetry of Robert Browning. Such anthology pieces as *How they brought the Good News*, *Marching Along*, *The Glove*, *A Grammarian's Funeral*, not to mention *Saul* and *Waring* had quenched any desire for a further acquaintance with his work. Consequently, when I saw that he was on the degree syllabus of the university with which I am associated, I breathed a deep sigh.

After some thought the prospect seemed brighter. At school I had also been inoculated against Conrad by a detailed examination study of *The Rover*, but Jocelyn Baynes' admirable work had brought me to understand and appreciate this great novelist. The same was true of F. R. Leavis's examination of Lawrence's *Women in Love*. I did not expect I should ever like Browning's poems; the working over of a select few of them by a 'Browning Lover' had been too thorough for that. I did expect to be relieved of any wide reading by discovering at least one excellent study of his poetry. This – with a few small personal additions – I could regurgitate, cormorant-wise, for my students. The precept 'Thou shalt not steal' is loosely interpreted in the academic world and if I could pick up some 'good thing' it need not be my own!

I was in for a sad disappointment. There was an exceedingly readable and well-documented biography of the poet by Mrs Betty Miller.[1] But for half a dozen worthwhile studies of Tennyson's poetry in a reasonable library there were perhaps two mediocre studies of Browning. And the critiques of Browning – I think of G. K. Chesterton and Dallas Kenmare – were not so much examinations of his work as rousing healths to the poet's noble sentiments and illustrious memory. Realizing my students had little stomach for such adulation, I turned without much hope to Stopford Brooke.

Brooke's study, published in 1902, was very much better. The language was not always to contemporary taste. There were such phrases as, 'this jovial monk [Lippo Lippi] . . . the secret of spring leaps in his veins . . . the poem seems as natural as the breaking forth of blossoms'. But Stopford Brooke had read deeply and with close attention. He provided an excellent résumé of Browning's last and unwieldy masterpiece, *The Ring and the Book*, he quoted well, and it was often possible to sweat down his effusions to remarks of real point and interest. Brooke set me reading the great monologues and love poems. It seemed obvious that such works as *Karshish*, *Cleon*, *Two in the Campagna*, or the *Invocation* to Elizabeth Barrett, were by a great poet. It was difficult to associate them with the jog-trot, facile verse which was my school diet of Browning. He is dead now and this may be a gross injustice, but it was equally difficult to believe that my schoolteacher who had enthused over the hearty simplifications of *Saul* and the *Rabbi Ben Ezra* was likely to have appreciated *Two in the Campagna* or the con-

[1] Betty Miller, *Robert Browning. A Portrait* (John Murray, 1952; Penguin Books, 1958).

18

clusion to *The Statue and the Bust* – if he had understood these works. I began to realize that the common gibe against Browning as the poet enjoyed by readers who do not enjoy poetry meant that many people only read his bad verse.

Much criticism merely repeats in contemporary terms the predilections of earlier critics as to a dead poet and their conceptions or misconceptions of his work. Because I am sure that no great poet is so misunderstood by our day and age as Robert Browning, I am glad that I read his poetry before I came across the recent examination of his life and work by J. M. Cohen.[1] Mr Cohen's book is efficiently written and constructed, but he applies to such minor verse as, for instance, *Christmas-Eve*, and to such a magnificent poem as *Childe Roland* the same unflinching approbation. This merely perpetuates the misconceptions about the work of a poet who has always suffered from his admirers. Mr Cohen does nothing to help the uncertain reader of our day who can only realize that *Childe Roland* is very good indeed if he understands that such poems as *Waring* and *Christmas-Eve* are thoroughly bad. However, Mr Cohen's book is well written. If I had not studied Browning's poems before I read it then I might have taken it for granted that *Saul* was a religious poem of the same quality as *Cleon* or *Caliban upon Setebos* and effectively insulated both myself and my students from any understanding of these works.

Saul has always been a favourite both of anthologists and critics. Browning's admirers have not been remarkable for their subtlety. Perhaps it is just their lack

[1] J. M. Cohen, *Robert Browning* (Longmans, 1952).

of subtlety which has attracted them to some aspects
of the poet, for when off-form he is a bird of the same
feather and shares their heavy obviousness of thought
and feeling. Time may well be in an acid in which bad
verse and bogus critical opinion dissolves, but the process is a lengthy one. Robert Browning has not yet
been dead for a hundred years and around his great
poems there is an exceptionally thick rind of bad work
for the acid of time.

One cannot judge a poem by the same resolute
criteria that serve for a brand of petrol or a detergent.
There is time, and there is the solitary communion of
the individual with a particular work. After reading
and re-reading *Two in the Campagna* and becoming
assured of its excellence, I turned for some confirmation of my response to L. G. Salinger's article on
Browning in *The Pelican Guide to English Literature*.[1]
My 'solitary communion' was badly shaken!

Salinger tells us, correctly enough, that Browning's
admiration for Donne was exceptional in his day and
is recalled by *Two in the Campagna*. He continues,
'But quite apart from the difference in sentiment, a
dramatic lyric by Donne has a tight progressive logic,
both on the plane of verbal reasoning and the psychological plane, whereas Browning's poems tend to fall
apart, so that he has to pull them together with a resounding exclamation. The good minute goes from the
poet as well as the lover.'

Little emerges from Mr Salinger's article except an
impression that any attempt to appreciate Browning is
considered bad academic form. I examine *Two in the*

[1] L. G. Salinger, 'Robert Browning', B. Ford, ed., *The Pelican
Guide to English Literature*, VI (Penguin Books, 1958).

Campagna in a later chapter and find it impossible not to believe it is a love poem of exceptional insight. There is no yardstick by which to judge a work of art, so this is a personal conviction. Mr Salinger's statement certainly provoked me to a 'resounding exclamation', but I can find no such loud empty noise in the conclusion of *Two in the Campagna*, a conclusion which clinches the whole argument of the poem.

This article convinced me that preconceptions which are entirely false come between the poems of Browning and their potential readers. One cannot be a Venerable Institution, a Board of Examiners, or that irritable god who flayed Marsygas for his presumption. One can develop a sincere admiration for a poet and believe that though misunderstood and unpopular much of his work is of great value. It is possible to support such a belief by quotation and comment, and point out the misinterpretation from which many of Browning's finest poems have suffered. It is also possible to highlight the verse, which, though admired by an earlier generation, is both false and copious enough to screen present-day readers from the poet's real achievement. This I have tried to do.

The task does seem important. An image has been imposed on the life and work of Browning. It applies both to his detractors and admirers. It bears little relevance to a poet whose insight into the relationship between the natural and supernatural worlds, men, women, and the polarities of good and evil, should be of exceptional interest to this age.

Chapter One

His Life and Present Reputation

I

The injury, dominated, is an asset;
It is there for domination, that is all.
Else what must faith do, deserted by mountains?
DAVID WRIGHT
Monologue of a Deaf Man.[1]

Robert Browning was born in Camberwell on May 7, 1812, three years after the birth of Tennyson and six years after the birth of his future wife, Elizabeth Barrett. His father, Robert Browning, was a bank clerk, bibliophile and scholar. Poets, like all other people, are profoundly influenced by their early upbringing. I suggested in an earlier book of mine, *The Price of an Eye*,[2] that if they possess the mysterious aptitude we call 'talent' then their upbringing may determine their vocation. However, neither the complexity of human nature nor the heart of a poet's mystery can ever receive more than the most partial explanation, whether it is couched in the terms of Freud, Jung or Karl Marx.

[1] From title poem (André Deutsch, 1958).
[2] Longmans (1961).

Not Chaos, not
The darkest pit of lowest Erebus,
Nor aught of blinder vacancy, scooped out
By help of dreams – can breed such fear and awe
As fall upon us often when we look
Into our Minds, into the Mind of Man . . .

That statement from Wordsworth's *Excursion*[1] is a welcome corrective to those writers who feel that a poet's human and creative complexity can be unravelled, neatly docketed and explained away in terms of their pet theory. I stress this because perhaps the best biography of Browning is by Mrs Betty Miller.[2]

Her book is extremely lively and informative; but it has a strong Freudian bias and is written with a determination to present a neat case history in Freudian terms. Like D. H. Lawrence Browning was extremely dependent upon his pious mother. He loved her so much he was once heard to say that even as a grown man he could not sit by her otherwise than with one arm round her waist. 'My room,' he wrote, 'is near hers and the door is left ajar.' So long as he lived in the same house as his mother he suffered, he tells us, 'very uncertain spirits'. No doubt Mrs Miller is correct in suggesting that this hypochondria came from an identification with Mrs Browning. The poet's letters to Elizabeth Barrett give ample evidence for such an identification. 'I will write tomorrow . . . the stupid head will not be quiet today – my mother is sadly affected too . . . I am quite well today and my mother is quite well . . . I am not too well this morning and write with an aching head. My mother's suffering continues too.'

[1] Preface to the edition of 1814.
[2] *Robert Browning. A Portrait, op. cit.*

24

But as David Wright says in the lines quoted at the head of this chapter, 'The injury, dominated, is an asset'. What matters and what it seems to me Mrs Miller tends to overlook is both the extent to which Browning, like D. H. Lawrence, transcended his fixation, and the use he made of it. She rightly stresses the great influence of Shelley upon the youthful Browning. He seemed to find in *Queen Mab*, in *Prometheus*, in *The Revolt of Islam* 'the key to a new world' and acknowledges his debt in *Pauline*:[1]

> I threw myself
> To meet it, I was vowed to liberty,
> Men were to be as gods and earth as heaven,
> And I – ah, what a life was mine to prove!
> My whole soul rose to meet it. Now, Pauline,
> I shall go mad, if I recall that time!

Shelley's influence was real enough. But when Mrs Miller writes, 'it is a measure both of the quality of his admiration for Shelley and the strength of his love for his mother, that his sanity was based on a consistent suppression of everything connected with "that time" ', then one has doubts!

Mothers – *Sons and Lovers* makes this point – may be difficult to outgrow, but Shelley although a potent first influence is unlikely to maintain the same hold throughout a life-time on any poetry lover let alone on a major poet. Surely Browning had to work through and slough off the influence of Shelley if his own gifts were to develop? To Mrs Miller, however, Browning's rejection of Shelley is not an inevitable stage of his poetic development but a betrayal.

[1] *Pauline; a Fragment of a Confession* (1833).

25

The ideals of Shelley and those of Sarah Anne Browning could not continue to exist under the same roof; the moment had come in which he must either deny his 'wild dreams of beauty and of good', or irreparably wound and alienate his mother. . . . Faced with this deadlock between head and heart, Browning found his own solution. Reason [presumably that faculty which should have bound him to the woolly atheistic humanism of Queen Mab!] divided him from the one being he could love [are we to assume he did not 'love' Elizabeth Barrett?]: reason, therefore, must be sacrificed.

It is surely remarkable that such an intelligent and scholarly biographer as Mrs Miller is able to believe that the author of *Karshish*, *Cleon*, or *The Ring and the Book* had dispensed with reason. Equally remarkable is her conception that the poet who wrote *The Statue and the Bust*[1] had surrendered his true convictions to an outworn and alien puritanism. Are we to assume that Sarah Anne Browning would have approved of her son's arraignment of conventional morality in this poem, and

> . . . the sin I impute to each frustrate ghost

> was, the unlit lamp and the ungirt loin . . .

applauded his conclusion that in certain circumstances it is not adultery which is immoral but conformity to moral precepts which bear no relevance to a particular human situation?

The critic and biographer must have a reasonably open mind if he is to present the life and work of a poet with some truth and amplitude. We all distort

[1] *Men and Women*, 1855.

reality by imposing upon it our preconceptions. But it is a question of degree; a strongly opinionated critic will either ignore those qualities of a poet which do not fit in with his opinions or distort them so that they will fit. Mrs Miller is fascinated by Browning but it is difficult not to believe that she has lopped and twisted both his life and work so that they will fit the Procrustean bed of her preconceptions. In *Psychoanalysis and the Unconscious*,[1] D. H. Lawrence writes that the 'mind provides us with a means to adjust to the materio-mechanical universe to our great end of creative life. And it gives us plain indications of how to avoid falling into automatism, hints for the applying of the will, the loosening of false, automatic fixations, the brave adherence to a profound soul-impulse. The mind as author and director of life is anathema.'

Lawrence's statement is not dissimilar to remarks made by Browning in a letter of 1876 to Mrs Fitz-Gerald, 'What strikes me so much in the life of Schopenhauer which you gave me, was the doctrine which he considered his grand discovery and which I have been persuaded of *from my boyhood* – that the soul is above and behind the intellect, which is merely its servant.'

Mrs Miller quotes this remark of Browning in her biography, but to support her belief that the young poet surrendered his intellectual and critical acumen in order to 'keep in' with Mrs Browning. Her condemnation of Browning's remark suggests that she considers a concern with religious experience and the use of the word 'soul' as an abnegation of Reason and this is supported by the scant attention she pays to his great religious poetry. It is also relevant that the poet says he

[1] 1921 (Heinemann ed., 1961).

27

believed from boyhood that the intellect is the servant of the soul since Mrs Miller suggests this belief only came out of his conflict as a young man – with mother!

It is difficult to associate the inspired vagaries of Shelley's life and work, not to mention his erratic navigation, with Reason. Nevertheless we are told that in discarding Shelley, Browning discarded intellect. 'Forcibly, in the course of this struggle, reason was dethroned . . . "to LOVE" became, thenceforward more important than "to KNOW".' Mrs Miller clinches her argument by an inventory of some of the items of the Browning estate, the property of the poet's son, sold by auction in London in 1913. Among these items 'was a small weightless object, carefully wrapped and labelled. It was a flower plucked from Shelley's grave.'

If the dead are to be judged by such minutiae no wonder Browning when alive had a profound suspicion of his future biographers.

The point is what the poet made of his overdependence on a redoubtable mother. From it he created such a penetrating study of fixation as *Andrea del Sarto* and *My Last Duchess*, a poem of exceptional insight into the sadistic domination which may result from self-doubt and inferiority. It is facile to construct a fantasy about an existence in which the hero and heroine 'live happily ever after'. It is surprising to find Mrs Miller subscribing to this idyll and finding in another of the poet's great achievements, *Two in the Campagna*, not a celebration of marriage and an acceptance of its inevitable limitations, but a statement of despair and disillusion. However she comments on this poem, 'Browning was filled with a desperate longing for the unimpaired communion of happier days'.

When 'Mum', no doubt, was in Heaven, and all right with the world! For my part I am doubtful whether marriage or any finite experience is a universal panacea and prefer to believe with Browning that though foxes have holes, etc., the son of man, since he is 'continued in our next', must remain unsatisfied – whatever the voltage of connubial or maternal bliss.

However, Mrs Miller is correct in pointing out Browning's dependence on his mother though she underestimates the use he made of it and the extent to which he overcame his fixation. No doubt one of the reasons for this fixation was the unusual passivity of the poet's father, a man who undoubtedly did allow himself to be dominated by his formidable if kindly wife, even to the extent of a weekly attendance at her Congregational chapel. Such a form of worship Mrs Miller suggests would hardly be congenial to a man 'who appreciated the wit of Voltaire and the subversive sting of Bernard de Mandeville'. Perhaps Mr Browning's passivity may have been related to some terrifying experience he had endured when in early life he was in charge of slave labour on the Island of St Kitts.

I have never known more of those circumstances, in his youth, than I told you [wrote Browning to Elizabeth Barrett] in consequence of his invincible repugnance to allude to the matter – and I have a fancy, to account for some peculiarities in him, which connects them with some abominable early experience. Thus – if you question him about it, he shuts his eyes involuntarily and shows exactly the same marks of loathing that may be noticed while a piece of cruelty is mentioned . . . and the *word* 'blood', even, makes him change colour.

29

It may well be that some horror of violence, both within himself and the world, was accentuated by this traumatic early experience and accounted for Mr Browning's extreme passivity. Although described by a friend as 'gentle as a gentle woman', Mrs Miller points out that he spent considerable time drawing 'grim heads', and masks in red chalk that were 'malevolent' and 'agonised'. Artists, one suspects, are driven to work out, make conscious and clarify those emotional conflicts that their parents have repressed. It is significant that the son of this man who feared his own violence, should have written poems which explore with exceptional insight the darkness and savagery which is part of our human condition.

Throughout his life, Robert Browning followed no other vocation than poetry. This, as I suggest later, may explain the uneven quality of his work. Despite this lack of a conventional involvement with the everyday world, Browning did not give his contemporaries the impression of being either shy or retiring but of considerable self confidence. He needed every scrap of it for from 1833, the date of the publication of *Pauline*, to 1861, the date of his wife's death, his poetry suffered almost thirty years of sustained neglect. That he showed only delight in the constant success of his wife's work which went into numerous editions, while his own was remaindered with a monotonous regularity, is not, I suspect, evidence of repressed envy on the part of the poet, but of the understanding and mutual tolerance of their marriage. One thinks of Hallam and Tennyson, of the support given by Coleridge and Dorothy to Wordsworth during the poet's many years of self-doubt and anxiety. Certainly, throughout their sixteen years of married life, Elizabeth supported, understood and constantly affirmed her husband's poetry. She realized that whereas her work came out of talent, his had the power of genius. It is significant that her death coincided with some recognition by the British public of this genius, and that deprived of the inspiration of his wife and the solitude she could create for him, Browning produced only one more great work, *The Ring and the Book*, which was published in 1869. After that we have twenty years of industrious versifying and dining out – but very little poetry.

Elizabeth Barrett was already well known as a poet when Robert Browning after reading her works wrote to her, 'I do, as I say, love these books with all my heart – and I love you too.' The declaration was not so much impetuous as a precognition of the affinity which existed between himself and this woman who was to give him a great deal of irritation, but also the love and understanding which was to enable him to write his finest poetry. What he gave her was nothing less than life itself; for the way Browning freed Elizabeth Barrett from a neurotic illness which had almost entirely abstracted her from everyday existence and brought her into marriage, motherhood and a life which was often both strenuous and absorbing, is close to miracle and myth.

The story has often been told. Although a passionate, violent and sensitive girl, after adolescence Elizabeth had withdrawn further and further into isolation and neurotic illness, her only contact with sanity and the everyday world being letters and her poetry. No doubt this withdrawal was caused by her father Mr Moulton Barrett, who was both a widower and a paranoid.

Mental and emotional aberration could reach an exceptional fullness and ferocity in the age which preceded the birth of psychotherapy! Certainly Mr Barrett's domination of his children was thorough and illuminated by no spark of insight. Any gesture of independence by these unfortunates was both criminal and a manifestation of monstrous ingratitude; marriage, or suggestion of marriage by either a son or a daughter, a heinous crime. Elizabeth was the most deeply involved with his insane possessiveness. No doubt it was the incestuous undertones of his relationship with his daughter which led Mr Barrett to cultivate her illness and withdrawal from the world of affairs. She must be his possession and imprisoned in her bedroom – which had of course an adjoining door to that of Papa. It was a mutual huddle. Late at night Mr Moulton Barrett would approach his daughter's bedside. 'Papa', she wrote, 'is my chaplain – prays with me every night – not out of a book, but simply and warmly at once – with one of my hands held in his and nobody besides him and me in the room.' During her Wimpole Street imprisonment the only noise that had 'the power of quickening my pulse' was the sound of her 'father's footstep on the stair and of his voice when he prayed in this room: my best hope, as I have told him since, being to die beneath his eyes'. That room has been admirably described by Mrs Miller. There was a double door to keep out the draughts and for seven or eight months of the year the edges of the windows were pasted over for the same purpose. Indeed Miss Barrett must have had a constitution of iron to live in the place at all for the oxygen supply was not only vitiated by her constant presence but the fact that both her sister Arabel and her spaniel Flush slept in the room. There is a vivid description of the winter condition of the place in a letter that she wrote to Miss Mitford. 'The consequence of living through the winter in one room, with a fire, day and night, and every crevice sealed up close; you may imagine perhaps by the help of your ideal of all dustlessness latent and developed. At last we come to walk upon a substance like white sand, and if we don't lift our feet gently up and put them gently down, we act Simoons and stir up the sand into a cloud . . . The spiders have grown tame – and their webs are part of our own domestic economy, – Flush eschews walking under the bed.' It was from this room and this spider's web of neurotic illness that Browning extricated his future wife. With infinite patience he taught her to walk and gave her back with his love her will to go on living. 'I have been drawn back into life, by your means and for you,' she wrote, 'I have come back for you alone . . . I have come back to live a little for you.'

The wonderful letters were written, the intimacy confirmed by meeting after meeting, and finally Elizabeth was strong enough to defy her overpowering father. The wedding took place on April 13, 1846, in St Marylebone Parish Church. Robert was thirty-three at the time and Elizabeth thirty-nine. Some six months later they eloped to Italy where they lived for the greater part of their sixteen years of married life. Elizabeth was free of her prison in Wimpole Street though she bitterly regretted her father's refusal ever to see her again or open her letters. His intransigence was quite his most creative attitude as a parent. Imagination boggles at the squalls the ferocious old gentleman would have created if he had paid the odd visit to his daughter and son-in-law.

The story of their married life is uneventful. The work went on, the understanding grew, there were friendships and expeditions to the Italian lakes and mountains. Elizabeth who had for years considered herself a bedridden invalid walked and rode on mules through the mountains; and on March 9, 1849, gave birth to their only child, Robert Wiedemann Barrett, whom they nicknamed Pen or Penini.

Successful though they were in their relationship with each other and in their work, with Pen the Brownings showed neither insight nor intelligence, only that curious local blindness which often disfigures the parenthood of men and women of genius. Elizabeth lavished on her unfortunate son a maternal affection which in its very excessiveness was narcissistic. She also projected on to him certain unresolved emotional conflicts connected no doubt with her own love-hate relationship with Mr Barrett. I do not believe this unresolved conflict contaminated her relationship with her husband, but it certainly played hell with Penini. One can only surmise whether the attritions of her paranoid father had given Elizabeth some unconscious hatred of maleness. But the fact remains that she dressed her son in smocks which even in that expansive age were remarkable for their decoration and frippery. She also cultivated the unfortunate boy's hair into such long and elaborate ringlets that passers by could not control their curiosity as to the little creature's sex, and when informed burst into cries of astonishment. It is remarkable that two people who both in their work and relationship with each other showed such profound insight and intelligence should have been so obtuse with their child. That Robert did bitterly resent Pen's ringlets is shown by the fact that one of the first things he did after Elizabeth's death was to take the boy to a barber. But by then the damage was done. No doubt Browning's inability to take a stand against his wife's treatment of Pen is connected with a hangover of his relationship with his mother. The letters give ample evidence of a curious passivity to Elizabeth. 'I submit to you,' he writes in 1845, 'and will obey you implicitly – obey what I am able to conceive of your least desire, much more of your expressed wish.' And in January, 1846, 'So take me and make me what you will – and though never to be more yours, yet more like you I may and must be, Yes, indeed – best only love.' I believe that his marriage enabled him to go beyond the somewhat abject dependence of those letters written during his courtship and that he did in fact achieve that degree of independence which is a condition of any successful marriage. On the other hand, though he could at times be assertive with Elizabeth – over her taste for spiritualism for instance and the medium Douglas Home – he could not take a stand over Pen. Perhaps it was his own unresolved motherfixation which made it impossible for Browning to say 'no' when night after night Pen was taken into the maternal bed, or do something to stem the excess of emotional stimulation to which the boy was subjected. Pen's destructive identification with his mother is perhaps suggested by what Browning wrote about the boy's behaviour immediately after Elizabeth's death, 'Pen has been perfect to me, he sate all day with his arms round me, *said things like her to me.*' The boy was ground between the millstones of genius. Although brisk enough with street girls, he was unable to consummate his own marriage, a fact which led his wife to enter an Anglican order. Pen himself did show some talent for painting and had exhibitions whose financial success was no doubt connected with his by then famous father. He also spent a great deal of time improving the family villa at Florence in which he installed both a new system of plumbing and a shrine to his dead mother.

There were occasional visits to London and Paris. Their circle of friends grew but was not allowed to intrude on the solitude and intimacy of their marriage. Robert, however, would very often leave his wife when they were staying in Rome and take part in numerous social activities, a foretaste of the incessant dining out of his later life. A description of the poet by Nathaniel Hawthorne in 1860, the last year of his marriage, gives an impression of health, confidence and exuberant energy. Browning 'seemed to be in all parts of the room at once and in every group at the same moment; a most vivid and quick-thoughted person, logical and common-sensible, as I presume poets generally are in their daily talk'. But Hawthorne's wife, Mrs Miller tells us, detected ' "an anxious line" on the poet's brow.' 'Nothing', she wrote, 'could resist the powerful impetus of his mind and heart, and yet this effervescing, resplendent life – fresh every moment like a waterfall or a river – seems to have a shadow over it, like a light cloud, as if he were perplexed in the disposal of his forces.' Mrs Hawthorne also divined Elizabeth Barrett's unwillingness to go on living. 'Only a great love', she wrote, 'has kept her on earth a season longer.' In her fifty-sixth year the contrast between Elizabeth and Robert was striking. Her hair was still long and black, but her face was shrunken and scorched with pain. Robert, however, in his fiftieth year was plump, bearded and genial. Loving her husband deeply, Elizabeth yet realized that she had, for all his devotion, become something of a burden. 'As for me,' she wrote bitterly to Browning's sister, Sarianna, 'I know my place, I am good only for a drag chain.'

Her death came to her on June 29, 1861, and is described by Browning in a letter to his sister Sarianna.

I called Annunziata, bade her get hot water as the doctor had done. I bade her sit up for the water. She did with little help – smiling, letting us act, and repeating, 'Well, you do make an exaggerated case of it!' 'My hands too?' she said and put them in another basin. I said 'You know me?' 'My Robert – my heavens, my beloved' kissing me (but I can't tell you) she said 'Our lives are held by God.' I asked 'Will you take jelly for my sake?' 'Yes.' I brought a saucerful and fed it by spoonfuls into her mouth. I then brought a second, and poured some into a glass – she took all. She put her arms around me – 'God bless you' repeatedly, – kissing me with such vehemence that when I laid her down, she continued to kiss the air with her lips, and several times raised her own hands and kissed them; I said 'Are you comfortable?' 'Beautiful'; I only put in a thing or two out of the many in my heart. Then she motioned to have her hands sponged – some of the jelly annoying her; this was done, and she began to sleep again – the last, I saw. I felt she must be raised, took her in my arms, I felt the struggle to cough begin, and end unavailingly – no pain, no sigh – only a quiet sight. Her head fell on me. I thought she might have fainted, but presently there was the least knitting of the brows, and A. cried 'Quest' anima beneditta e passata!'

It was so. She is with God, who takes from me the life of my life in one sense – not so in the truest. My life is fixed and sure now.

So ended the temporal manifestation of the most important experience of Browning's life. George Santayana wrote, 'We tend to think of life as an entertainment or a spectacle; in point of fact it is an ordeal'. That Browning's relationship with his wife implied conflict and difficulty is witnessed by his own words.

The general impression of the past [he wrote a few years later] is as if it had been pain. I would not live it over again, not one day of it. Yet all that seems my real *life* – and before and after, nothing at all; I look back on all my life when I look *there*: and life is painful. I always think of this when I read the Odyssey – Homer makes the surviving Greeks, whenever they refer to Troy, just say of it 'At Troy, where the Greeks suffered so.' Yet all their life was in that ten years at Troy.

After his wife's death, Browning lived mainly in London with occasional visits to Brittany and – after 1878 – to Italy. His brisk but – as regards poetry – posthumous existence is described by Henry James in his story *The Private Life*. James found it hard to reconcile 'the loud, sound, normal, hearty presence, all so assertive and so whole, all bristling with prompt responses and expected opinions and usual views', with the great poet. For after *The Ring and the Book* although he wrote much garrulous, didactic, optimistic verse, Browning ceased for the most part to write poetry. Without inspiration his energy was taken up

38

by argument, dining out and friendships with intelligent women, to none of whom would he surrender his independence or fidelity to Elizabeth by entering into marriage. Like Wordsworth, when he read aloud his earlier poetry he gave the impression that he was reading the work of another man.

The essence of Browning's life was in his marriage, and the best account of that marriage is his love poetry which I will discuss in my second chapter. In the meantime I want to suggest some reasons for the extraordinary variations in the quality of this great poet's work; variations which exist during his most creative years.

II

No poet has merited the term 'great' with greater reservations than Robert Browning. That the author of *Childe Roland, Karshish, Two in the Campagna* or *The Ring and the Book* could perpetrate such doggerel as *Waring*, such banal religiosity as *Christmas-Eve* and such abject sentimentality as *A Lover's Quarrel*, is one of the great paradoxes of literature.

It is true that the quality of Tennyson's poems is also extremely variable. But with Tennyson the variation is usually in the quality of separate poems; between *The Ode on the Duke of Wellington*, for instance, and *Rifleman Form*, between *Mariana* and *O Darling Room*. With Browning the cleavage often exists in the same poem. *Popularity*,[1] despite T. S. Eliot's statement that 'Tennyson and Browning are poets, and

[1] *Men and Women.*

they think, but they do not feel their thought',[1] does seem to me to have something of that condensed and intellectual passion which we find in the best metaphysical verse. It is, in part, an examination of artistic process. In order to gain the raw experience for his work the artist descends into the depths of himself like the fishermen of Tyre who dived for certain shells from which was made a valuable blue dye.

> I'll say – a fisher (on the sand
>   By Tyre the Old) his ocean-plunder,
> A netful, brought to land.
>
> Who has not heard how Tyrian shells
>   Enclosed the blue, that dye of dyes
> Whereof one drop worked miracles,
>   And coloured like Astarte's eyes
> Raw silk the merchant sells?

But the raw shellfish is of no more intrinsic value than the poet's experience unrefined by art. Experience and fish must both be worked upon with the greatest skill if the dye and the work of art is to be created.

> Mere conchs! not fit for warp or woof!
>   Till art comes, – comes to pound and squeeze
> And clarify, – refines to proof
>   The liquor filtered by degrees,
> While the world stands aloof.

Once an original artist has made the perilous descent into the depths of himself, and transmuted that experience into a work of art, then

> . . . there's the extract, flasked and fine,
>   And priced, and saleable at last!

[1] Selected Essays, *The Metaphysical Poets*, 287 (Faber, 1932).

The last two verses with their terse and ironic wit are not irrelevant to our own decade with its obsession for the artistic gimmick. The artist creates out of his experience and skill a new way of knowing and seeing. Simply because his vision is new, it is not immediately accepted and he may gain neither understanding nor material reward. But gradually his vision does percolate through into human consciousness and then he is followed by a shoal of imitators who without having paid his price for experience and without possessing his skill turn out watered-down variations on his great themes, and achieve material prosperity.

> . . . Hobbs, Nobbs, Stokes and Nokes combine
>   To paint the future from the past,
> Put blue into their line.
>
> Hobbs hints blue, – straight he turtle eats.
>   Nobbs prints blue, – claret crowns his cup.
> Nokes outdares Stokes in azure feats, –
>   Both gorge. Who fished the murex up?
> What porridge had John Keats?

Popularity is by no means one of Browning's greatest poems, but it has wit and intelligence, and at times an ease of movement and splendour of imagery comparable to the poetry of Yeats. In this description of the miraculous dye, for example, and its abundance:

> Enough to furnish Solomon
>   Such hangings for his cedar-house,
> That when gold-robed he took the throne
>   In that abyss of blue, the Spouse
> Might swear his presence shone
>
> Most like the centre-spike of gold
>   Which burns deep in the blue-bell's womb,

What time, with ardours manifold,
  The bee goes singing to her groom,
Drunken and overbold.

Some trouble is starting in that stanza! It requires a certain ingenuity to accept a 'groom with a womb'! But on the whole there is both imagination and technical skill in this examination of artistic process. That is why the contrived rhyme of stanza eight sticks out like a sore thumb.

Yet there's the dye, – in that rough mesh,
  The sea has only just o'er-whispered!
Live whelks, the lip's-beard dripping fresh,
  As if they still the water's lisp heard
Through foam the rock-weeds thresh.

'O'er-whispered' and 'lisp heard' jolt the poem to a full stop. How, one asks, with the whole work almost perfectly there, could Browning have let that clever bit of nonsense through? There is no definite answer. One can say that this poet had at times an extraordinary insensitivity to rhyme values; a kind of rhyming phobia which found a perverse pleasure in making unholy marriages between quite unrelated pieces of language. Ingenuity of rhyme is, however, a mark of light verse and the gaiety of *The Pied Piper of Hamelin*[1] is inseparable from its ingenious rhymes. The Mayor, for instance,

(Nor brighter was his eye, nor moister
Than a too-long-opened oyster,
Save when at noon his paunch grew mutinous
For a plate of turtle green and glutinous) . . .

[1] *Dramatic Lyrics and Romances* (1842–5).

But for the most part the rhyming phobia occurs when Browning is not really involved with his theme, and is either being didactic or melodramatic. That doggerel verse sermon *Christmas-Eve* contains very little of Browning's genius but some of his worst rhymes – 'compressed and coalesced', for example, 'flightier and mightier', 'fruition and apparition'. Sometimes a poem in which Browning does seem to be involved is choked to death by perversities of rhyme. This is the case in *A Grammarian's Funeral*,[1] where we have such associations – and they are typical – as 'cock-crow' and 'rock row', 'fabric' and 'dab brick', 'premature' and 'profit, sure'.

Ernest Hemingway said that an essential requisite of any writer was 'an inbuilt shock-proof shit-detector'. Browning's 'detector' was more fallible than any other poet of stature – with the possible exception of Wordsworth. One has to reconcile works which contain such monstrous marriages as 'failure' and 'pale lure' or 'Bishop' and 'Fish up' with the extreme technical skill of such a masterpiece as *My Last Duchess*. In this work the full rhyming couplets are unnoticeable, so perfectly do they express the exact tone of voice and human flavour of the protagonist, the hysteria which lies under the Duke's frigid formality. But it is in later chapters that I will examine the great merit of so many of Browning's poems. At the moment I want to throw some light on the rubbish which undoubtedly does exist, and has been used both to obscure and dismiss this great poet's real achievement.

It is difficult to separate a poet's technique and his sensibility. Where Browning's technique is clumsy

[1] *Men and Women.*

then his thought is usually heavily didactic and his sensibility crude or mawkish. One can pardon, even enjoy, this passage from *A Lover's Quarrel*;[1] the pre-Freudian age was less selfconscious than our own about such off-beat erotic excursions.

> Teach me to flirt a fan
> As the Spanish ladies can,
>   Or I tint your lip
>   With a burnt stick's tip
> And you turn into such a man!
>   Just the two spots that span
> Half the bill of the young male swan.

But what can one make of the poem's rousing conclusion?

> It is twelve o'clock:
> I shall hear her knock
> In the worst of a storm's uproar,
>   I shall pull her through the door,
> I shall have her for evermore!

It is not remarkable that this raw and infantile grasping should have been felt by Robert Browning. Most of us carry some unresolved detritus of childhood over with us into later age. It is remarkable that a poet who at about the same time was writing *Two in the Campagna*, one of the most mature and thoughtful love poems in the language, should have let those sentiments loose on the printed page.

The point, as I suggested in my first chapter, is the deep cleavage within Browning and that unlike other great and divided artists – Baudelaire, one thinks of, perhaps W. B. Yeats – this cleavage expresses itself in

[1] *Dramatic Lyrics* (1842).

the poetry. The variation between his good and bad work is a question of personality. But it was enhanced by the pressures of Browning's particular age and is a characteristic of other Victorian poets. It is connected with the remarkable bulk of their work and with the fact that they felt themselves to be dedicated bards in the Wordsworthian tradition. In an age of intense productivity and moral obligation, they felt they had a duty to produce. So did John Donne, perhaps, Milton, Vaughan, Traherne, Blake and Wordsworth. But in the case of the last two poets, Blake, throughout a lifetime, Wordsworth in his great ten or so years, wrote in comparative solitude, and with their eyes turned not to a reading public – that would exist in the future – but to their inner daemon, the world of their inspiration. The eyes of Browning and Tennyson were cocked all too often towards a reading public. When inspiration was at a loss, they tended to give this public not what they as poets really knew and felt about the human predicament but what they knew the public felt they ought to feel. That is one reason for the exceptionally thick rind of dull, sentimental and didactic verse which surrounds the poetry of these men.

Another lies in the lack of inspiration. Inspiration is a rare visitor and comes in its own good time, not by industry or at a word of command. Wordsworth had no other vocation but that of the poet, yet he only kept up poetry for ten years; the rest of his life was spent for the most part in industrious versifying. Blake had to earn his living as an engraver. Chaucer, Donne, Milton and Marvell were all involved in making a living and the world of affairs. This meant that they had something to do when they had no inspiration, that their attention was not constantly screwed up to poetic creation. One cannot think of John Donne's wife, or Milton's 'late espoused saint' writing to some eminent friend for 'some pretty witty, tender, little thing, that dear John can turn into a copy of verses!' Yet such was Mrs Tennyson's plea, a heartfelt one too, because when deserted by either his personal Muse or, public a-Muse, the poet could create hell at Farringford. A poet needs some external interest to weld him into everyday life, provide the grit of experience, and keep him busy when he has no inspiration and consequently no excuse for trying to write a poem; except in the sense of that expectant and effortful waiting and discarding which is a condition of poetry. Of course, for many verse writers, particularly of the 18th century, there is no distinction between verse and a daily chore; but the visionary poet does seem to need that involvement with life one associates with a job as part of his more important vocation.

No doubt Baudelaire's angst and syphilis were as effective in keeping his work clear of rubbish as a post in the Board of Trade. All Browning had was Elizabeth Barrett. Out of his relationship with that woman, out of the solitude they created together, came some of his greatest poetry. But she was not enough to keep him busy when he had nothing to say, nor were the dinner parties, the modelling in clay, the reproduction of old masters. So, since to put it flippantly, 'Satan finds some mischief still for idle hands to do', he turned out the mass of bad verse which screens our generation from his greatest poetry.

Undoubtedly the stuff went down as well as if not

better than poetry. Just as the Victorian public appreciated the sentimentality and jingoism of Tennyson, so, once they got round to it, they thoroughly enjoyed the didactic and facile sermonizing of Browning.

This is one reason for the present neglect of the poet. Another is that we have only recently emerged from the reaction against Victoriana. Yet, though Browning's great contemporary is eminently Victorian, Tennyson has been rehabilitated for some years, and besides excellent studies by Harold Nicolson and J. H. Buckley,[1] received the accolades of W. H. Auden and T. S. Eliot. Certainly with his controlled anxiety, his sense of the finite human being menaced by the impersonal processes of time and the unchartered energies of the unconscious, his tension between religious doubt and affirmation, Tennyson though of his own perplexed age has much to say to our own. But with the exception of the startling and seldom mentioned *Lucretius*, his work is not particularly disturbing or provocative of any re-examination of oneself and the time-ingrained habits of thought. Perhaps that is why his stock – after a temporary fall – is again high on the literary 'Change'.

Browning's work is disturbing in its examination of man, society and religious experience. Moreover, his best poems are surrounded by enough bad verse to give critics – who do not as a rule wish to be disturbed by poetry – a good excuse for writing off his work as a total loss. Such anthology pieces as *Saul, Christmas-Eve, Waring* and *Rabbi Ben Ezra*, attract the insensitive reader and seem to justify Browning's dismissal

[1] Harold Nicolson, *Tennyson* (Constable, 1923); J. H. Buckley, *Tennyson* (Harvard and Oxford University Press, 1960).

as a minor and rather vulgar writer. It is also unfortunate that in certain moods the poet will coarsen some of his most sincere convictions by a kind of hearty simplification. In *Bishop Blougram's Apology*,[1] an uneven poem which I will discuss in a later chapter, there is such a simplification of Browning's belief that the soul grows and gains strength out of pain and conflict.

> No, when the fight begins within himself,
> A man's worth something. God stoops o'er his head,
> Satan looks up between his feet – both tug –
> He's left, himself, in the middle: the soul wakes . . .

The sporting imagery of that passage is quite inappropriate to the spiritual theme, though it would have delighted James Thurber!

The commonplace work of Browning has attracted commonplace critics. The best work of Browning has been largely neglected, perhaps because it is disturbing, because it insists on asking questions and will not be passive material for the scalpel of analysis. His poetry examines in depth the motivation of human behaviour. It scrutinized those philosophical and religious formulae and habits of thought which often explain away rather than elucidate the mystery of existence. Because it explores the human being in depth and questions conventions of morality and behaviour, Browning's great poetry can elicit from the reader a self reappraisal which may be both arduous and disturbing.

[1] *Men and Women.*

Chapter Two

His Love Poetry

I

You creature with the eyes!
From *Pippa Passes*.[1]

In *Two in the Campagna*,[2] ~~one of his finest poems~~,
Browning writes about the inevitable duality of human
existence in relationship to his love for Elizabeth
Barrett.

> The champaign with its endless fleece
>   Of feathery grasses everywhere!
> Silence and passion, joy and peace,
>   An everlasting wash of air —
> Rome's ghost since her decease.
>
> Such life there, through such lengths of hours,
>   Such miracles performed in play,
> Such primal naked forms of flowers,
>   Such letting Nature have her way
> While Heaven looks from its towers.

This is an assertion of the goodness of sensuality.
Nature has her way under the eye of Heaven because,

[1] 1841.   [2] *Men and Women.*

49

How say you? Let us, O my dove,
    Let us be unashamed of soul,
As earth lies bare to heaven above.
    How is it under our control
To love or not to love?

There is no disharmony between the claims of earth
and heaven, spirit and flesh. Like Blake, Browning believes they are manifestations of a single energy.

'Man has no Body distinct from his Soul; for that
call'd Body is a portion of Soul discern'd by the five
Senses, the chief inlets of Soul in this age.'[1] Yet like
all human experience, though with a special intensity,
love reveals its impasse. It suggests an at-oneness between a man and a woman which in point of fact can
never be completely realized. Duality must remain,
the separateness of one self, the otherness of the other.
However satisfying the communion, it can never
wholly absorb our desire which must go on beyond
any human relationship.

I would that you were all to me,
    You that are just so much, no more –
Nor yours, nor mine, – nor slave nor free!
    Where does the fault lie? what the core
Of the wound, since wound must be?

The 'wound' and the 'fault' are a condition of our
'fallen' humanity. We are involved in both a finite and
infinite scheme of existence. We are circumscribed by
our ego and everyday awareness and yet touch over
into 'unknown modes of being'. Our desire for knowledge and experience must exceed the reach of our in-

[1] William Blake, 'The Voice of the Devil' (*The Marriage of
Heaven and Hell*, 1793).

telligence and five senses. Like St Peter on the Mount of Transfiguration we have our moments of timeless communion but 'then the good minute goes' and we are involved once more in time, dissatisfaction, or the merely 'common' good of existence.

> Already how am I so far
>   Out of that minute? Must I go
> Still like the thistle-ball, no bar,
>   Onward, whenever light winds blow,
> Fixed by no friendly star?
>
> **Just when I seemed about to learn!**
>   **Where is the thread now? Off again!**
> **The old trick! Only I discern –**
>   **Infinite passion and the pain**
> **Of finite hearts that yearn.**

'Off again! the old trick!' Browning increases the emotive force of his poem by setting against its visionary statements such flat almost cynical phrases; the ironic 'shrug' which is a characteristic of modern poetry.

Love can yield that cleansed perception which enables us to see the infinite in another person, but we cannot hold to this perception. Indeed, as Blake says, it is destructive to try and do so.

> He who binds to himself a joy
> Does the winged life destroy;
> But he who kisses a joy as it flies
> Lives in eternity's sun rise.[1]

We have our moments of limitless vision and timeless communion but for all that we remain divided creatures, limited in our capacity to know and love.

[1] *Eternity* (*Verses and Songs* from the Rossetti and Pickering MSS).

All we can do is recognize the division; it is this recognition which makes the division fruitful.

(*Two in the Campagna* seems to me Browning's greatest love poem. It has an exceptional maturity, not only because it celebrates married love, that is to say a love relationship which has to some extent been proved real by time and purged of fantasies, but because the poem both affirms the reality of love and admits its limitations.)The impasse that is implicit in this experience cannot be solved by argument, only by the acceptance of 'being', and the continuity of a life which is shared however imperfectly. This is the theme of *A Woman's Last Word*.[1]

> Let's contend no more, Love,
>   Strive nor weep –
> All be as before, Love,
>   – Only sleep!
>
> What so wild as words are?
>   – I and thou
> In debate, as birds are,
>   Hawk on bough!
>
> See the creature stalking
>   While we speak –
> Hush and hide the talking,
>   Cheek on cheek!
>
> What so false as truth is,
>   False to thee?
> Where the serpent's tooth is,
>   Shun the tree –
>
> Where the apple reddens
>   Never pry –

[1] *Men and Women.*

> Lest we lose our Edens,
> Eve and I!

The woman's desire to avoid the tree does not suggest a disbelief in the value of understanding but a realization of its limitations. Here we see 'through a glass darkly' and can achieve no complete knowledge or final answer. The attempt to find such an answer substitutes 'knowing' for 'being'; George Meredith realized it was a cause of the breakdown of his marriage.

> Their hearts held cravings for the buried day.
> Then each applied to each that fatal knife,
> Deep questioning, which probes to endless dole.
> Ah, what a dusty answer gets the soul
> When hot for certainties in this our life![1]

The *Invocation* to his dead wife at the end of Book I of *The Ring and the Book*[2] is a tremendous affirmation of Browning's faith that 'Love's not time's fool', and that relationship can in some mysterious way both continue and grow between the living and the dead.

> O lyric Love, half-angel and half-bird
> And all a wonder and a wild desire, –
> Boldest of hearts that ever braved the sun,
> Took sanctuary within the holier blue,
> And sang a kindred soul out to his face, –
> Yet human at the red-ripe of the heart –
> When the first summons from the darkling earth
> Reached thee amid thy chambers, blanched their blue,
> And bared them of the glory – to drop down,
> To toil for man, to suffer or to die, –
> This is the same voice: can thy soul know change?
> Hail then, and hearken from the realms of help!

[1] *Modern Love* (1862), final poem.   [2] 1868.

Never may I commence my song, my due
To God who best taught song by gift of thee,
Except with bent head and beseeching hand –
That still, despite the distance and the dark,
What was, again may be; some interchange
Of grace, some splendour once thy very thought,
Some benediction anciently thy smile:
– Never conclude, but raising hand and head
Thither where eyes, that cannot reach, yet yearn
For all hope, all sustainment, all reward,
Their utmost up and on, – so blessing back
In those thy. realms of help, that heaven thy home,
Some whiteness which, I judge, thy face makes proud,
Some wanness where, I think, thy foot may fall!

Although he holds to her humanity 'yet human at the red-ripe of the heart', Browning invests his wife with the more than human significance that Dylan Thomas in his poem *After the Funeral, In Memory of Ann Jones*,[1] gives to his dead aunt

> Her flesh was meek as milk, but this skyward statue
> With the wild breast and blessed and giant skull
>
> . . . .
>
> These cloud-sopped, marble hands, this monumental
> Argument of the hewn voice, gesture and psalm,
> Storm me forever over her grave . . .

The poem makes the same affirmation of the soul's existence before birth that we find in Wordsworth's *Immortality Ode* and such poems of Yeats as *Mohini Chattergee* or his play *Purgatory*. Elizabeth, 'Boldest of hearts that ever braved the sun', that is to say temporal existence, had taken 'sanctuary within the holier blue' of a timeless world. She is summoned back to the

[1] *Collected Poems* (Dent, 1952).

'darkling earth' for the work that God requires of her. It is significant that in this last great poem of Browning he admits how much of the inspiration he owes to Elizabeth.

> Never may I commence my song, my due
> To God who best taught song by gift of thee . . .

He also says in the extremely evocative and condensed last lines of this *Invocation* that death has not really divided him from his wife and that he can still write with her help and understanding. Perhaps this communion did exist as he wrote *The Ring and the Book*. Certainly it is the last of Browning's great poems and although he turned out a great deal of amorous verse in later life, inspired by his relationship with various women admirers, it has little value. Only in one later poem does something of the old passion break out. Again it is a question of Elizabeth.

TO EDWARD FITZGERALD[1]

> I chanced upon a new book yesterday:
> I opened it, and where my finger lay
>   'Twixt page and uncut page these words I read
> – Some six or seven at most – and learned thereby
> That you, FitzGerald, whom by ear and eye
>   She never knew, 'thanked God my wife was dead.'
>
> Ay, dead! and were yourself alive, good Fitz,
> How to return you thanks would task my wits:
>   Kicking you seems the common lot of curs –
> While more appropriate greeting lends you grace:
> Surely to spit there glorifies your face –
>   Spitting – from lips once sanctified by Hers.

[1] Miscellaneous poems, 1870–89.

In the poems I have been discussing and such works as *By the Fire-side* and *One Word More*, Browning considers love as a creative and sustaining experience although he realizes its contradictions and difficulties. But many of his poems treat of its darker side, of the possessiveness and frustration which can overshadow marriage. This is not surprising since Browning's own marriage was real and consequently not merely a question of sweetness and light. It is often his unresolved conflict which becomes the theme of a writer, rather than the serene and integrated elements of his personality. For just as the Holy Ghost delivered St Thomas Aquinas from a multitude of opinions, so the free flow of existence may deliver us from talking and writing about those aspects of our lives which have achieved some wholeness and serenity. The 'solved' experience by the very fact that it is solved dispenses with examination or the need for resolution. It is the unsolved experience that solicits understanding, and that is why so much European literature attempts to let light on conflict and confusion. Perhaps it is also why there are so very few good paintings of the Resurrection of Christ although we have innumerable fine interpretations of his Crucifixion. Miss Stevie Smith may be right when she suggests there will be no literature in Heaven! Her 'Mrs Arbuthnot' incidentally, is a dead poetess who to her sorrow was deserted by inspiration in later life!

> Mrs Arbuthnot has died,
> She has gone to heaven,
> She is one of the heavenly combers now
> And need not write about them,
> Cry! She is a heavenly comber,
> She runs with a comb of fire,

Nobody writes or wishes to
Who is one with their desire.[1]

A considerable part of the work of any writer will often
centre round those problems which he finds it most
difficult to solve in his personal life. Browning's extreme reticence and dislike of autobiographical confession is expressed in a poem called *House*.[2]

'Hoity toity! A street to explore,
  Your house the exception! "*With this same key
Shakespeare unlocked his heart*," once more!'
  Did Shakespeare? If so, the less Shakespeare he!

But despite this reticence Browning's letters and such
biographical detail as Mrs Miller has collected make it
plain that he had an unusual dependence on his wife.
Friends, for instance, were astonished that even in late
years he grew uncomfortable if not sitting next to her
during an evening out. It is lucky that Elizabeth
Barrett was deeply attached to her husband and
attached in a way which, I believe, for the most part
fostered his poetry and independence. Otherwise his
tendency to fixation might have led to sterility both in
the life and the work. As it is, his wife may well have
helped him to understand his dependence and put it to
poetic use. Certainly he has written with exceptional
insight about fixation; I mean a relationship between
men and women where love is not a means of fulfilment but a form of slavery. In *The Clod and the Pebble*
Blake expresses the creative and destructive polarity of
this relationship.

[1] Stevie Smith, *Mrs Arbuthnot* (*The Frog Prince*, Longmans,
1966).
[2] *Pacchiarotto and Other Poems* (1876).

ROBERT BROWNING

'Love seeketh not Itself to please,
Nor for itself hath any care,
But for another gives its ease,
And builds a Heaven in Hell's despair.'

So sung a little Clod of Clay
Trodden with the cattle's feet
But a Pebble of the brook
Warbled out these metres meet:

'Love seeketh only Self to please,
To bind another to Its delight,
Joys in another's loss of ease,
And builds a Hell in Heaven's despite.'[1]

Some of Browning's most interesting poems are on the theme of that last verse. The pebble is a person whose insecurity, masked by an unfeeling hardness, cannot tolerate the independence of another human being. Otherness and individuality are a threat which such people do not meet by deepening their capacity to feel and know until the threat is absorbed by a communion which is greater than the anxiety of separation. On the contrary they attempt to reduce their partner to servitude. It is a kind of psychological vampirism. It seeks for slavery and destroys relationship since it denies that separate personality which is an essential condition of dialogue and meeting. The logical conclusion of this desire for total possession is a species of necrophilia, intercourse of one kind or another with a human who has been reduced to a thing. It is this intention though with no particular insight that peers ghoulishly through the romantic trappings of *Porphyria's Lover*.[2]

[1] *Songs of Experience* (1789–94).
[2] *Madhouse Cells* (*Poems*, 1849).

58

A girl comes to her lover at night, who very briskly strangles her because he realizes that 'the good minute goes' and finds intolerable the unease which her humanity – a ghostly and unpredictable energy – causes him.

> Be sure I looked up at her eyes
> > Proud, very proud; at last I knew
> Porphyria worshipped me; surprise
> > Made my heart swell, and still it grew
> While I debated what to do.
> That moment she was mine, mine, fair,
> > Perfectly pure and good: I found
> A thing to do, and all her hair
> > In one long yellow string I wound
> Three times her little throat around,
> And strangled her.

It is interesting that such an odd little study of psychopathology should have found its way into so many anthologies. The emotions behind it seem unleavened by insight and have the same case-book quality that we find in the first series of Swinburne's *Poems and Ballads. My Last Duchess*[1] is also concerned with this theme. But here Browning shows extreme insight into the insecurity which leads to sadistic domination. A Renaissance duke is negotiating his second marriage to the daughter of a neighbouring count. He is talking to a representative of this count who has been sent to arrange the terms of marriage. At the start of the monologue he draws back a curtain and shows a picture of his last wife who 'died'.

[1] *Poems, ibid.*

> That's my last Duchess painted on the wall,
> Looking as if she were alive; I call
> That piece a wonder . . .

With great skill Browning reveals to the reader both the process by which the Duke stifled his wife's will to live and the fact that he does not realize the cruelty of his behaviour but believes that he has acted with propriety as a great nobleman and husband. The portrait he gives of his wife reveals a woman with that spontaneity and innocence which Blake associates with the unfallen soul.

> She had
> A heart . . . how shall I say? . . . too soon made glad,
> Too easily impressed; she liked whate'er
> She looked on, and her looks went everywhere.
> Sir, 'twas all one! My favor at her breast,
> The dropping of the daylight in the West,
> The bough of cherries some officious fool
> Broke in the orchard for her, the white mule
> She rode with round the terrace – all and each
> Would draw from her alike the approving speech,
> Or blush, at least.

But it is the very 'goodness' of the Duchess, her capacity to respond deeply to all creation that repels the Duke. A predator, who strives to fill the vacuum of himself with the personality of another, he feels cheated by her delight in all living creatures. That delight should be occasioned by himself only and to his jealous eye her impersonal love seems personal infidelity.

> She thanked men, – good; but thanked
> Somehow . . . I know not how . . . as if she ranked

My gift of a nine hundred years old name
With anybody's gift. Who'd stoop to blame
This sort of trifling? Even had you skill
In speech — (which I have not) — to make your will
Quite clear to such an one, and say 'Just this
Or that in you disgusts me; here you miss,
Or there exceed the mark' — and if she let
Herself be lessoned so, nor plainly set
Her wits to yours, forsooth, and made excuse,
— E'en then would be some stooping, and I chuse
Never to stoop.

The ease of this monologue disguises its extreme compression. The poem is only about sixty lines in length, but Browning charges the words with such suggestiveness that they evoke in the mind of the reader an enormous complexity of situation, action and character. The innumerable possibilities, for instance, of those 'commands' by which the Duke stifled his wife's will to live are all the more sinister for being unspecified.

Oh, Sir, she smiled, no doubt,
Whene'er I passed her; but who passed without
Much the same smile? This grew; I gave commands;
Then all smiles stopped together.

There is no overt condemnation in the poem, only a presentation of personality and conduct, and it is clinched by the final lines which make it clear that to the Duke a human being must be possessed like a bronze statue and that this will be the fate of his next Duchess.

Nay, we'll go
Together down, Sir! Notice Neptune, tho',
Taming a sea-horse, thought a rarity,
Which Claus of Innsbruck cast in bronze for me.

61

The conflict is between the innocent and the corrupt, between evil and good, and it is my belief that Browning explored it as fully as any writer of his age. How can someone who feels spontaneously and is therefore vulnerable survive those onslaughts which Louis MacNeice writes about in his *Prayer before Birth*?[1]

I am not yet born; O hear me,
Let not the man who is beast or who thinks he is God come
    near me.

I am not yet born; O fill me
With strength against those who would freeze my
    humanity, would dragoon me into a lethal automaton,
      would make me a cog in a machine, a thing with
        one face, a thing, and against all those
          who would dissipate my entirety, would
            blow me like thistledown hither and
              thither or hither and thither
                like water held in the
                  hands would spill me
Let them not make me a stone and let them not spill me.
Otherwise kill me.

The same conflict between an intrinsically good, uncorrupted vitality and an authority, associated with rank and power, which is parasitic on the life it attempts to dominate, is the theme of an early poem, *The Flight of the Duchess*.[2] It was written before Browning's marriage to Elizabeth Barrett, but it is difficult not to associate the rescue of the poem's heroine by the gypsies with the poet's rescue of his wife from neurotic illness and her father.

Although an important poem, *The Flight of the Duchess* has a lightness of tone which to some extent

[1] Faber, 1944.   [2] *Dramatic Lyrics and Romances.*

justifies a number of fantastic rhymes – 'hirsute' and 'fur suit' for instance, or 'helicat' and 'delicate'.

It has the exuberance and suggestiveness of a good fairy story and something of the compression and psychological insight of a short story by D. H. Lawrence. The Duke is another 'hollow man', his virility contaminated by his mother, 'the tall, sick yellow Duchess'. As a climax to his attempts to subject his wife, 'she was active, stirring, all fire', to the deathly régime of his household, the Duke tries to make her take part in a ceremony which under its 'quaint and folkish' surface is a symbolic desecration of life itself. There is going to be a stag hunt.

> Now you must know, that when the first dizziness
> Of flap-hats and buff-coats and jackboots subsided,
> The Duke put this question, 'The Duke's part provided,
> Had not the Duchess some share in the business?'
> For out of the mouth of two or three witnesses,
> Did he establish all fit-or-unfitnesses:
> And, after much laying of heads together,
> Somebody's cap got a notable feather
> By the announcement with proper unction
> That he had discovered the lady's function;
> Since ancient authors held this tenet,
> 'When horns wind a mort and the deer is at siege,
> Let the dame of the Castle prick forth on her jennet,
> And with water to wash the hands of her liege
> In a clean ewer with a fair toweling,
> Let her preside at the disemboweling.'

Unaware that she possesses just the imagination and free vitality which he detests, the Duke sends an old gypsy woman to his wife. Her decrepitude is to be a kind of sermon, a *memento mori*, and bring the

Duchess to her senses. Actually the old gypsy, a character invested by Browning with sybilline power and dignity, gives the Duchess the confidence to escape with the gypsies from her husband's intolerable household.

There is no escape for *Andrea del Sarto*,[1] and unlike the other victims of love he is imprisoned, not by the economics of marriage, but by his obsession for a destructive woman. As so often in Browning's monologues he is both a man and a type. Fra Lippo Lippi, the protagonist of another poem, represents, besides his own exuberant humanity, the first break away of Renaissance art from those diagrams of spiritual tranquillity and aspiration which achieved their perfection in Giotto, a break away to imaginative naturalism. The painter Andrea del Sarto expresses the decline of this naturalism into an obsessive and unimaginative concern with form, perspective and proportion; at least in some of his less significant pictures. Like the twilight greyness of so much of his work, Andrea's life is sterile. He married, Vasari tells us, a woman called Lucrezia who destroyed both his reputation and artistic capacity. The poem is a superb portrait of obsession, of a man who willingly accepts his bondage to a woman who he knows quite well is unfaithful to him and exploits him both morally and financially. That Del Sarto was well aware of his wife's character is shown by his fine portrait of Lucrezia in the Prado Museum of Madrid. The face has a certain beauty but is mean and predatory.

> My serpentining beauty, rounds on rounds!
> – How could you ever prick those perfect ears,

[1] *Men and Women.*

> Even to put the pearl there! oh, so sweet –
> My face, my moon, my everybody's moon . . .

The qualification of 'moon' by the possessive adjective 'everybody's' suggests not only that her beauty sheds light on all the world, but her promiscuity, which the painter is well aware of. Browning makes Andrea's resigned acceptance of his wife's infidelity all the more moving by the subtle restraint of its presentation. She has been wheedling money out of her husband to give to a fictitious cousin from the country whom Andrea knows to be her lover. The somewhat unholy twilight communion of the painter and his Lucrezia is punctuated by 'noises off', a soft whistle from this impatient lover. The poem ends: 'Again the Cousin's whistle! Go, my Love.'

This is not a poem of information but of knowledge, and Browning was able to achieve this intimacy between himself and the dead Florentine painter because he himself had a capacity for fixation. 'The injury', I quote David Wright again, 'dominated, is an asset; It is there for domination, that is all.'

The tension, implicit in Browning's relationship with Elizabeth Barrett, indeed between most men and women of any sensibility, is expressed in *Any Wife to Any Husband*,[1] a poem which, though both moving and extremely interesting, is unsuccessful in that Browning is not able to do real justice to his theme or to solve the problems it poses. Like the dying bishop of St Praxed[2] the wife of this poem is mediating at the

---

[1] *Men and Women.*
[2] *The Bishop Orders His Tomb at St Praxed's Church* (*Dramatic Lyrics and Romances*).

point of death and like the bishop, though with infinitely greater subtlety, she projects or imposes temporal values on to the dimension of death and eternity.
'Because our inmost beings met and mixed,' the woman
believes that she has achieved in her marriage with her
husband a singular at-oneness. This at-oneness will
survive death and bodily decrepitude.

> But the soul
> Whence the love comes, all ravage leaves that whole;
> Vainly the flesh fades – soul makes all things new.

But although the wife believes she has this spiritual
affinity with her husband, that they have in Yeats's
words 'halved a soul', their unity may be cheapened by
the claims of the flesh, that is to say by the erotic relationships which she divines her husband will make
with other women after her death.

> Is the remainder of the way so long
> Thou need'st the little solace, thou the strong?
> Watch out thy watch, let weak ones doze and dream!

> ' – Ah, but the fresher faces! Is it true,'
> Thou'lt ask, 'some eyes are beautiful and new?
> Some hair, – how can one choose but grasp such wealth?
> And if a man would press his lips to lips
> Fresh as the wilding hedge-rose-cup there slips
> The dew-drop out of, must it be by stealth?'

The confusion one finds in this poem between temporal and eternal values produces conclusions which
are both interesting and a trifle bizarre. For instance
the wife believes that she and her husband have
achieved a deep and indestructible union. It is real and
will survive death, but despite it her husband will have

erotic relationships with other women. Consequently from where she sits and watches – it is characteristic of the poem that the spiritual entity should both 'sit' and 'watch' – she will not only see her husband making love to other women but, since she is one with him, have to participate in his love making.

> So must I see, from where I sit and watch,
> My own self sell myself, my hand attach
> Its warrant to the very thefts from me . . .

In fact, though the poem is technically very fine, deeply felt and of considerable psychological interest, Browning is not so much coping with its problem as circling round it. The problem as so often with him, is the relationship of individuality to eternity, more specifically of the spiritual and physical marriage of two people to that dimension. It is the same problem that the Sadducees put to Christ.

There were therefore seven brethren: and the first took a wife, and died without children. And the second took her to wife, and he died childless. And the third took her; and in like manner the seven also: and they left no children, and died. Last of all the woman died also. Therefore in the resurrection whose wife of them is she? for seven had her to wife.

And Christ states that the finite laws of temporal existence do not apply to death.

And Jesus answering said unto them, The children of this world marry, and are given in marriage: But they which shall be accounted worthy to obtain that world, and the resurrection from the dead, neither marry. nor are given in marriage: neither can they die any more: for they are equal unto the angels; and are the children of God, being the children of the resurrection.[1]

That is, I suspect, the definitive answer to such a question. But the wife of this poem, like the dying bishop of St Praxed, cannot let go her hold on temporal life and its values. For all the pathos of her meditation there is possessive jealousy in it; jealousy not so far removed from that which prompted the richer partners of many marriages to 'bind another' from beyond the grave; to stipulate for example that in the event of their spouse's remarriage all money should pass to the children or a cats' home. Her fantasy of having to take part at one remove in her husband's liaison with another woman resembles in its refusal to accept the sea-change of death the dying bishop's conviction that he will as a spirit derive considerable pleasure from contemplating a large lump of semi-precious stone poised between the knees of his skeleton.

> Some lump, ah God, of *lapis lazuli*,
> Big as a Jew's head cut off at the nape,
> Blue as a vein o'er the Madonna's breast . . .
> .   .   .   .
> So, let the blue lump poise between my knees,
> Like God the Father's globe on both his hands
> Ye worship in the Jesu Church so gay,
> For Gandolf shall not choose but see and burst!

That is a vigorous statement by a man with little or no spiritual perception. The woman has much insight. But although it has made her aware of the significance of her relationship with her husband and the fact they

[1] Luke, 20, 29–36, Authorized Version, reprinted by permission.

have met in some area of being beyond the finite ego
it has not enabled her to realize that such a meeting
can neither be contaminated nor destroyed since it
exists, and 'where neither moth nor rust doth corrupt'. Their relationship in eternity she sees as an extension of their relationship in time, and as such it
will be affected by temporal contacts.

> Why must I, 'twixt the leaves of coronal,
>   Put any kiss of pardon on thy brow?
> Why need the other women know so much
> And talk together, 'Such the look and such
>   The smile he used to love with, then as now!'

But at times the poem does achieve the certainty of
faith, that leap of the imagination by which the human
being is able to bridge the gap between life and death.
This verse, for instance, has something of the urgency
and serenity of Bishop King's Exequy for his dead
wife:

> Re-coin thyself and give it them to spend, –
> It all comes to the same thing at the end,
>   Since mine thou wast, mine art, and mine shalt be,
> Faithful or faithless, sealing up the sum
> Or lavish of my treasure, thou must come
>   Back to the heart's place here I keep for thee!

One measure of the stature of a poet is the capacity
of his work to offer varied and significant meaning to
succeeding generations of readers. That is why there
are innumerable critiques of Shakespeare. There is no
definitive meaning. There is the meaning which satisfies and is therefore true – for a particular age. That
meaning may either be incomprehensible or a platitude to another.

Throughout this book I have selected those poems of Browning for examination which seem to me most interesting. I hope that because I am alive now this also means that these poems have some especial relevance to my own day and age. The bland optimism of 'they lived happily ever after' is not an appropriate attitude to marriage for this day and age. Nor could Shakespeare's *Othello* or Strindberg's *The Father* have been written in this age of psychology.

I mean for the post-Freudian generation both *Othello* and *The Father* have to some extent ceased to be tragic heroes and become 'cases'. 'Put out the light and then put out the light'; the magnificent poetry cannot have quite the same significance to an age that is familiar with unconscious motivation and realizes that they are uttered by a someone who though stricken and heroic is about to suffocate his wife with a pillow because of paranoid delusions.

I suggest that Browning's poems about marriage are of particular interest today because he does not romanticize either the good or evil implicit in the relationship. In such poems as *Andrea del Sarto* or *My Last Duchess* he shows us how destructive marriage can become. But the destructiveness is never exaggerated or glamorized; it is examined and understood, and with that knowledge of unconscious motivation which pervades our present time. Again, in his poems which celebrate the goodness of marriage, *Two in the Campagna*, for instance, or *A Woman's Last Word*, he does not celebrate some idyllic fantasy, but what is; I mean both the joys – they are incomplete – and the difficulties – they can be negotiated – which are the essence of any meeting.

70

II

With the notable exception of *The Ring and the Book*, and the sonnet to FitzGerald, Browning's work, after his wife's death is garrulous and uninspired. One long poem, *Ferishtah's Fancies*, published in 1884 when the poet was over seventy and famous, throws some light on the failure of his inspiration. It contains a number of love lyrics which, although of little value in themselves, do show up by their uncertainty and blurred sentiment both the virtues of Browning's finest love poetry and his predicament in later age – a predicament which is anticipated by *Any Wife to Any Husband*. Certainly it is hard to believe that these poems come from such deep feeling as gives an edge to the sexual poems written by Yeats when he was over sixty. The wisdom, passion and nostalgia of Yeats's later work depends, in part, on the fact that when he finally broke away from his fixation to Maud Gonne and could give himself to a love that was reciprocated, he was an ageing man. Browning's later poems do not seem the expression of a new and passionate involvement with a woman. Nor are they merely the hangover of his marriage to Elizabeth Barrett although that relationship overshadowed his later life. Despite the poet's chronological age at the time of their composition, some of the lyrics of *Ferishtah's Fancies* express a callow, somewhat strident sensuality and a lack of insight which could be associated with adolescence. To say that the sexual poetry of Browning's sixties and seventies is adolescent is not to deny that his marriage to Elizabeth Barrett was for the most part exacting and mature, or that he celebrated it in some of the finest love poetry of our language. It is to say that one may by-pass a certain stage of maturation and as a result be haunted in later age by what one has failed to live through in youth. In later years Browning had still a debt to pay to life. It is this unpaid debt that made it difficult for him to pass beyond Eros and find themes more appropriate to his sixth and seventh decade than current opinion or sexual compulsiveness.

In the powerful tenth lyric of *Ferishtah's Fancies* the poet seems to regress from a development he had achieved in earlier years, to deny the insight he had gained from marriage.

> Eyes shall meet eyes and find no eyes between,
>   Lips feed on lips, no other lips to fear!
> No past, no future – so thine arms but screen
>   The present from surprise! not there, 'tis here –
> Not then, 'tis now: – back, memories that intrude!
> Make, Love, the universe our solitude,
> And, over all the rest, oblivion roll –
>   Sense quenching Soul!

'Back memories that intrude', 'No past, no future – so thine arms but screen the present from surprise'. Somewhat desperately Browning is trying to wrench himself away from his involvement with his wife; an involvement which, as he affirms in his *Invocation* to Elizabeth in *The Ring and the Book*, because of its insight and intensity could not end with death. He denies in this lyric the duality which he had affirmed in earlier poems as an essential condition of marriage. Since his deeper emotions are still tied up with his dead wife, 'sense must extinguish soul'. Sense is not, as in *Two in the Campagna*, a means by which soul can express itself. Browning is reversing the order affirmed in his great poetry; Body is no longer an attribute of the Psyche, the Psyche is within the Body like a pin in a pin-cushion, or how could 'Sense quench Soul'?

However in the Epilogue to *Ferishtah's Fancies*, almost, one feels, against his conscious intention, Browning does affirm the supreme importance of his relationship with Elizabeth. For the most part the poem is a vision of the Makers, those men and women who have given to life without stint and with little desire for external reward. It starts in a mood of troubled uncertainty, then, in the beautiful second verse, the vision breaks through Browning's unease:

Only, when I do hear, sudden circle round me
— Much as when the moon's might frees a space from
    cloud —
Iridescent splendours: gloom — would else confound me —
    Barriered off and banished far — bright-edged the blackest
    shroud!

Unfortunately when 'the famous ones' actually speak it is in that over-optimistic somewhat hectoring tone which mars much of Browning's later work and reaches its climax in the Epilogue to *Asolando* which exhorts us 'to greet the unseen with a cheer'. In the present poem we are told:

Then the cloud-rift broadens, spanning earth that's under,
    Wide our world displays its worth, man's strife and strife's
    success:
All the good and beauty, wonder crowning wonder,
    Till my heart and soul applaud perfection, nothing less.

73

However the whole tone of the poem is changed by its conclusion. The loud optimism serves as a device (though this may not have been Browning's intention) to give added point and seriousness to the quiet statement that fame and material or artistic success are irrelevant, a veil of enchantment over what really matters – our capacity to make a deep and lasting relationship with another human being.

> Only, at heart's utmost joy and triumph, terror
> Sudden turns the blood to ice: a chill wind disencharms
> All the late enchantment! What if all be error –
> If the halo irised round my head were, Love, thine arms?

Despite himself Browning is affirming the dialogue with his wife which had kept him open to the source of his poetry.

Although marriage confirmed his belief that individual growth, indeed salvation itself, depended upon a specific meeting with a unique person of the opposite sex, Browning had held this belief for some years before he met Elizabeth Barrett. For Plato the original state of the unfallen soul was androgynous. Sexual longing could be explained by the desire of the half soul to regain wholeness by uniting with its male or female counterpart. But Plato did not believe such a union could in itself produce wholeness; that depended upon individual development, and the pains of growing – often in solitude. Browning seems, at times, to affirm that a person of the opposite sex can actually be one's lost spiritual counterpart. In this sense love and marriage are the fulfilment of destiny. *Cristina*,[1] a poem published three years before his meeting with

---

[1] *Dramatic Lyrics and Romances.*

Elizabeth Barrett, describes the brief and only partially fulfilled meeting between a man and a woman who are each other's destiny.

> There are flashes struck from midnights,
>   There are fire-flames noondays kindle,
> Whereby piled-up honors perish,
>   Whereby swoln ambitions dwindle,
> While just this or that poor impulse,
>   Which for once had play unstifled,
> Seems the sole work of a life-time
>   That away the rest have trifled.

What such moments reveal is the extreme importance of relationship. Learning to love is the point of temporal existence.

> Doubt you if, in some such moment,
>   As she fixed me, she felt clearly,
> Ages past the soul existed,
>   Here an age 'tis resting merely,
> And hence, fleets again for ages:
>   While the true end, sole and single,
> It stops here for is, this love-way,
>   With some other soul to mingle?

In *Cristina* Browning suggests that if the significance of the destined meeting is not realized then the chances of spiritual growth and integration may be lost, perhaps, forever. The soul

> '. . . loses what it lives for,
>   And eternally must lose it . . .'

It is not just a question of marriage or sexual intercourse but of realization, of being aware when the unique meeting occurs that one has encountered one's destiny within another person. Because the man in *Cristina* has understood that he possesses this special affinity with the woman the real purpose of his life has been completed.

> Such am I; the secret's mine now!
> She has lost me – I have gained her!
> Her soul's mine: and, thus, grown perfect,
> I shall pass my life's remainder,
> Life will just hold out the proving
> Both our powers, alone and blended –
> And then, come the next life quickly!
> This world's use will have been ended.

One's uncertainty both as to the woman's fate and the efficacy of so brief a meeting as a means to perfection suggests that in this poem Browning has not proved his Platonic conception in the mill of actual experience.

In *Evelyn Hope*,[1] a poem written towards the end of his marriage, the idea of meeting as destiny is worked out with much greater assurance. No doubt Browning is expressing some ambivalence to a wife six years his senior and prematurely aged by disease in this poem about a man who meets his destiny in a girl very much younger than himself. Certainly the awkwardness of a real relationship is neatly by-passed in 'Beautiful Evelyn Hope is dead' – killing off the heroine. But death may postpone, it cannot prevent the consummation in some further existence, of the destined meeting.

> No, indeed! for God above
> Is great to grant, as mighty to make,
> And creates the love to reward the love, –
> I claim you still, for my own love's sake!

[1] *Men and Women.*

Delayed it may be for more lives yet,
   Through worlds I shall traverse, not a few –
Much is to learn and much to forget
   Ere the time be come for taking you.

As in such poems of Yeats as *Mohini Chattergee*, Browning states here that the human spirit must work through life-cycle after life-cycle until it reaches fulfilment.

But if *Cristina* is immature then *Evelyn Hope* suffers from a certain incompleteness, as if Browning was not wholly committed to his theme, or not sufficiently conscious of the emotions that lay behind it. There is a note of sentimentality in the work, as if he was escaping into fantasy from the fact that his wife had, in some moments, become 'little better than a drag-chain'.

I say 'in some moments' because for all its tensions his marriage remained creative. Indeed the poet's most sincere statement of 'meeting as destiny' is made in *By the Fire-side*,[1] a poem which considers his relationship to his wife.

My own, confirm me! If I tread
   This path back, is it not in pride
To think how little I dreamed it led
   To an age so blest that by its side
Youth seems the waste instead!

My own, see where the years conduct!
   At first, 'twas something our two souls
Should mix as mists do: each is sucked
   Into each now; on, the new stream rolls,
Whatever rocks obstruct.

[1] *Men and Women.*

77

Despite the slightly unfortunate undertones of the
verb 'sucked', associating as it does a spiritual and
heterosexual relationship with the primal experience
of babyhood, this poem is successful. Since it is rooted
in experience Browning makes less resort to the innumerable question marks with which he peppers his
work when he is writing beyond his emotional means.
In the *Invocation* of *The Ring and the Book* he seeks
communion with his wife beyond death. In this poem
he enquires – but without stridency and so the question is its own answer – into their mutual fate after
death.

> Think, when our one soul understands
>   The great Word which makes all things new –
> When earth breaks up and Heaven expands –
>   How will the change strike me and you
> In the House not made with hands?

By the Fire-side celebrates the married communion by
which Browning believed he and his wife had fulfilled
their temporal destiny although the need for further
understanding and insight was without end.

> And to watch you sink by the fire-side now
>   Back again, as you mutely sit
> Musing by fire-light, that great brow
>   And the spirit-small hand propping it
> Yonder, my heart knows how!
>
> So the earth has gained by one man more,
>   And the gain of earth must be Heaven's gain too,
> And the whole is well worth thinking o'er
>   When the autumn comes: which I mean to do
> One day, as I said before.

Spiritual growth, Browning believed, depends on a heterosexual relationship with one specific person. In two poems, *Dîs Aliter Visum*[1] and *The Statue and the Bust*,[2] he examines the sterility and degeneration which may result if having been confronted by such a relationship it is rejected because of timidity or sloth.

Dîs Aliter Visum was written in 1864. It describes the meeting after an absence of ten years of a young woman and an old and fairly famous writer; two people who have ruined both themselves and others because although they shared a destiny they failed to fulfil it. Browning is writing at the height of his powers in this poem and makes his bitter appraisal of failure in the exact tones and rhythms of colloquial speech. This blend of colloquialism and deep seriousness is part of his contribution to the poetry of our own age. As they walk along the sea cliff the woman is talking to the man who should have been her lover and husband.

> While . . . do but follow the fishing-gull
> That flaps and floats from wave to cave!
> There's the sea-lover, fair my friend!
> What then? Be patient, mark and mend!
> Had you the making of your scull?

Ten years ago the ageing poet had rejected, indeed failed even to make articulate, the affinity which both he and the woman realized existed between them when they met and talked at the same resort. Browning makes the commonplace remarks of the verse expose the mistrust of instinct and spontaneity which led

---

[1] *Dîs Aliter Visum; or, Le Byron de nos Jours* (*Dramatis Personae*, 1864). The title ('But the gods thought otherwise') is from Virgil, *Aeneid*, Bk II.   [2] *Men and Women.*

the poet to deny the woman who was his destiny. 'The fishing-gull', 'the sea lover', is what she remarks on their walk; but the bird in its freedom and at-oneness with the sea is a bitter comment on the man, divorced as he is from the deeper reaches of himself and the truth of impulse. 'Had you the making of your scull?' His reason is a mere part of life and can create and control nothing. But he has tried by means of his intellectual will to control 'being', instead of using intellect and will to interpret its intentions. At their first meeting he should have trusted not reason alone, but the whole scope of his humanity.

> Thus were a match made, sure and fast,
>   'Mid the blue weed-flowers round the
>   mound . . .

He has shrunk back from the moment of truth and the fact that his reasons for withdrawal are thoroughly sound does not mitigate the failure which involves both himself and three other people. Here is the sensible reason:

> A match 'twixt me, bent, wigged and
>   lamed,
> Famous, however, for verse and worse . . .

> And this young beauty, round and sound
>   As a mountain-apple, youth and truth . . .

In the last verse Browning describes the result of merely *common* sense, the hopeless situation of these people who, having turned aside from their feeling towards each other, have destroyed their capacity to feel, and become parasites upon emotion. The poet is totally indifferent to his mistress, the woman bored with her husband.

For Stephanie sprained last night her wrist,
   Ankle or something. 'Pooh,' cry you?
At any rate she danced, all say,
   Vilely; her vogue has had his day.
Here comes my husband from his whist.

In the stanzas which precede this final verse the woman
condemns the facile rationalism of the poet. He has
sought for a 'balanced' life and failed to realize that the
essential quality of being human as opposed to animal
is incompleteness. Their very disparity of age was 'the
fruitful impasse' in which they might both have become more human, and transcended their humanity.
In his later work Browning is very often turning argument and idea into verse, although we feel they could
have been equally well expressed in prose. Here the
idea is realized in a superb image, and as such exists in
itself, and is irrefutable.

This you call wisdom? Thus you add
   Good unto good again, in vain?
You loved, with body worn and weak;
   I loved, with faculties to seek:
Were both loves worthless since ill-clad?

Let the mere star-fish in his vault
   Crawl in a wash of weed, indeed,
Rose-jacynth to his finger-tips:
   He, whole in body and soul, outstrips
Man, found with either in default.

But what's whole, can increase no more,
   Is dwarfed and dies, since here's its sphere.
The devil laughed at you in his sleeve!
   You knew not? That I well believe;
Or you had saved two souls: nay four.

81

The Statue and the Bust also examines the sterility of two people who have failed to implement their mutual destiny. As in *The Flight of the Duchess*, Browning uses in this poem something near to fairy story in order to express his convictions about human nature. It tells of a woman and a duke of Florence, who because of fear and sloth, postpone the meeting which was their destiny, until time and physical decrepitude take it out of their reach. Relationship is inconvenient and incompatible with conventional morality, so they reason it away — and are destroyed in the process. The woman becomes the picture she has put at the window in place of her ravaged face and frustrated instincts; the Duke becomes the bronze statue he has substituted for his passion. Almost until the end, this poem, though lively and well-made, remains a parable, almost a diagram through which the poet can express, at one remove, some of his deepest convictions. But in the last verse Browning comes out into the open. Where meeting is destiny, conventional morals are irrelevant.

> I hear your reproach — 'But delay was best,
> For their end was a crime!' — Oh, a crime will do
> As well, I reply, to serve for a test,
>
> As a virtue golden through and through,
> Sufficient to vindicate itself
> And prove its worth at a moment's view.

As Browning also affirms through Lazarus in *An Epistle of Karshish*[1] there is a morality of eternity which transcends that of time. Since these two people

[1] *An Epistle Containing the Strange Medical Experience of Karshish the Arab Physician* (*Men and Women*).

were each other's destiny they have sinned against
this timeless morality.

> The counter our lovers staked was lost
> As surely as if it were lawful coin:
> And the sin I impute to each frustrate ghost
>
> Was, the unlit lamp and the ungirt loin,
> Though the end in sight was a crime, I say.
> You of the virtue, (we issue join)
> How strive you? *De te, fabula!*

Having failed in life the protagonists of *The Statue and
the Bust* have gone, undeveloped, into Death. Negation
is not a virtue.

> So! while these wait the trump of doom,
> How do their spirits pass, I wonder,
> Nights and days in the narrow room?
>
> Still, I suppose, they sit and ponder
> What a gift life was, ages ago,
> Six steps out of the chapel yonder.

Action is of time, 'being' of eternity. But one's action
in time, or lack of it conditions one's being in eternity.
The frustrate ghosts of *The Statue and the Bust*, since
they failed to act in time, fail to 'be' in eternity.

> Surely they see not God, I know,
> Nor all that chivalry of His,
> The soldier-saints who, row on row,
>
> Burn upward each to his point of bliss —
> Since, the end of life being manifest,
> He had cut his way thro' the world to this.

One can only act rightly and do good through those
particular details of conduct which accord with one's

particular destiny. The destiny of the Duke and the woman cut across the dictates of current morality. Since meeting was their fate, their sin was 'the unlit lamp and the ungirt loin', disobedience to an intention of life which was greater than their individual personalities. Finally, *'De te fabula'* (this is your story), Browning broadens out his poem and makes it refer to a whole society which has let a part dictate to the whole, and turned against the instinctive and spiritual ground of temporal existence. In their varied ways, T. S. Eliot, Yeats and D. H. Lawrence make a not dissimilar diagnosis.

Chapter Three

Religious Poetry before Browning

'Long life and good health to your honour,' said he as he
turned away.

The Philosopher lit his pipe.

'We live as long as we are let,' said he, 'and we get the
health we deserve. Your salutation embodies a reflection on
death which is not philosophic. We must acquiesce in all
logical progressions. The merging of opposites is comple-
tion. Life runs to death as to its goal, and we should go
towards that next stage of experience either carelessly as
to what must be, or with a good, honest curiosity as to what
may be.'

'There's not much fun in being dead, sir,' said Meehawl.

'How do you know?' said the Philosopher.

JAMES STEPHENS
The Crock of Gold.[1]

Much significant poetry is religious. It may be a poetry
of doubt but it is religious in that it suggests that we
are involved in many dimensions of existence. We are
material entities living in a material world, and limited
by time and space. We are also a spiritual or psychic
process and as such not wholly circumscribed by time
and space and our perishing bodies but 'moving about
in worlds not realized', worlds which can only be

[1] Bk 1, *The Coming of Pan.*

understood in part by the finite intellect. Significant poetry, whatever its theme, usually suggests and, to some extent, examines this duality.

Although it may be possible to have direct knowledge both of ourselves and what mystics call 'the divine' ground of our being, it is difficult to communicate this knowledge to other people with any directness. To express his unique insight into the human soul Christ usually draws on counterparts and resemblances taken from the external world. The Prodigal Son, the Buried Talent, the Pearl, the Wedding Garment; the Gospels abound in such images for the inner life of man and the process of a second birth and self-transcendence. It is true that until recently we have taken these images far too literally and tended to see in the Prodigal Son, for instance, only a useful tract for the reformation of convicts. But through the works of such men as Jung and Maurice Nicoll, we are regaining an inward significance of Christ's sayings and beginning to free ourselves from the materialism of Nicodemus who could not understand a second birth through 'water and the spirit'. One may *know* God and the deeper reaches of the self, but this knowledge is of things unseen. As such it can only be communicated through things seen; that is to say through the images of religion and poetry.

Not even in such a prosaic statement as 'I would like another cup of tea' does language fully encompass the experience it attempts to communicate. The imagic language of great religious poetry keeps close to its theme, to the experience it is trying to communicate. However, it includes as part of its statement the suggestion that language can never wholly encompass the experience which it is striving to body forth. Visionary poetry admits that there must be a gap between words and what they are about, but it uses words in such a way that this very hiatus becomes part of the experience which words communicate. This is a form of humility and criticism can only do justice to such writing if it has a similar reticence. Later in this book I suggest that Browning's finest religious poetry does possess this virtue; in his bad verse it is absent.

Humility, the humility of reticence where reticence is required, gives to the utterances of religion and great poetry, if not a firmer approximation to the chimera of absolute truth than the statements of science, a greater capacity to continue to bear meaning. This endurance does not depend only on poetry and religion having as their theme certain psychological processes which are the perennial condition of humanity. Nor is it only a question of the ability of poetic language (the language of religion is usually poetic) to recreate the experience it describes, so that the words involve both our intellectual and emotional life. The point is that great poetic and religious statements include as part of what they say the inevitable gap between words and what words refer to. This enables such a statement to admit of many different interpretations while maintaining the essence of its original intention. The innumerable commentaries on the sayings of Christ – not to mention William Shakespeare – continue for the most part to bear some relevance to their theme. A poem, a poetic drama, a parable or aphorism can continue to offer significant if divergent meanings to successive decades. A merely didactic or dogmatic statement can be drained of meaning by a shift of opinion; a scientific proposition can be made invalid by further and incompatible information.

Browning's best religious poems have a reticence which is appropriate to their transcendental themes, and are capable of many interpretations. But there is a great gap between his good and bad religious verse, a gap which can only be understood if we examine some aspects of the religious poetry which preceded his age.

In the 17th century English religious poetry can be of the highest quality and in the Christian sense, orthodox. Milton, though of the century and a great poet, is outside the province of this book. He created an epic from the mythology of the Old Testament. In *Samson Agonistes* he arraigns and questions his God like an old servant who despite his devotion to his master has fallen on evil days. But Milton's work has little Christian significance in the sense of that humble and intimate communion with Christ, and God the Father which characterizes the work of Donne, Herbert, Vaughan, Traherne and Crashaw. Since the response of these poets to Christianity was of the whole man it included, particularly in the case of Donne, revolt and turbulence. But for all that their poetry and meditations were close to the doctrine and dogma of their church, whether it was Catholic or Anglican.

With the exception of Gerard Manley Hopkins, and some passages of T. S. Eliot, only in the 17th century do we find a large body of visionary poetry which is in harmony with orthodox Christianity. Towards the end of the 18th century great religious poetry is written again, by Blake and Wordsworth. Some of Blake's religious poems – this is unique in literature – make us feel that we are overhearing a lively and developing dialogue between the poet and the Christ of the

Gospels. So strong is this sense of intimacy that when he writes,

> I was standing by when Jesus died
> What they called humility I called pride . . .

we are inclined to believe Blake was present at the Crucifixion! But although Blake writes in a Christian tradition his interpretation of Christianity is unlikely to have endeared him to theologians. Wordsworth's *Immortality Ode* and many passages from *The Prelude* are of the greatest religious significance, but they are no more specifically Christian than the *Upanishads* or the *Bhagavad-Gita*. The same is true of much religious poetry of the Victorian age and our own.

Blake and Wordsworth begin a new and exploratory dialogue between man and whatever is signified by the word 'God'. Before this new dialogue starts, we have the 18th century. Since it sees the end of a form of conversation between man and God which had lasted for over a thousand years, as far as great religious poetry goes, the age is almost silent. A form of religious experience had come to an end. Interest had shifted from speculation as to the nature and operation of a First Cause to that detailed study of secondary causes which was pioneered by such men as Kepler, Galileo, Bacon, Harvey, Newton; a study which is characteristic of science. Scholastic 'evidence' for revealed truth and the dogmatic assertions of revealed truth we associate with scholasticism wilted before the accurate observation of natural phenomena which had begun in the 16th century.

On the outskirts of the age we do have those vital expressions of Christianity associated with Dissent, the

Journals of Fox, the hymns of Charles Wesley and
Isaac Watts. But as regards its most typical poets,
philosophers, and men of letters there is no living
dialogue between man and God, only formal conversation – polite and one-sided.

> The spacious firmament on high,
> With all the blue ethereal sky,
> And spangled heav'ns, a shining
>   frame,
> Their great Original proclaim.

Addison's well-known hymn affirms the belief of the
Augustan Age that men could know God through a
purely rational observation of 'Nature'. They considered 'Reason' as the supreme human faculty, and
associated the discovery of Reason, of mathematical
laws operating in Nature with 'absolute' truth. They
would have had scant regard for our own uncertainty
as to the scope of Mathematics; an uncertainty which
is implicit in Empedocles' definition of God 'as a circle
whose centre is everywhere and whose circumference
does not exist'. Reason could explain Nature in terms
of Mathematics. Consequently the Divine Original of
Nature was a great mathematician. Innumerable fac-
tors made this particular explanation into the one valid
explanation for the most representative men of the
Augustan Age. Since it was at the time satisfying, the
fact that an explanation which reduced Nature to a
'grand machine' and God to a 'grand mechanic' was
an immense belittlement of God and Nature, was not
apparent. It is apparent from Addison's hymn that
Deistic Rationalism seemed to have divorced God and
Nature.

What though in solemn silence all
Move round this dark terrestrial ball;
What though nor real voice nor
    sound
Amid their radiant orbs be found;
In reason's ear they all rejoice,
And utter forth a glorious voice,
Forever singing as they shine,
'The hand that made us is divine.'

There is 'nor real voice nor sound' in the universe, that is to say no possibility of man obtaining some direct experience of the Deity. However, it is that very Reason which has denied the *immanence* of God which fetches him back – as a First Cause. The mathematical laws men were discovering within the universe suggested that a Grand Mathematician had planned them. Since his 'Mechanism' was perfect he had no need to meddle with it. He could not be known by any spiritual or mystical insight; He could be inferred from his harmonious creation.

An inevitable result of the revolutionary scientism of the 18th century and the belief of this age that all significant truth could be discovered by rational observation was a belittlement of imagination, instinct, intuition, those faculties by which we may apprehend an order of being not accessible to the intellect. The new Science was too rewarding and absorbing for its exponents to realize that a denial of whatever is signified by 'Imagination' might imply a curtailment of our ability to comprehend whatever is signified by the word 'Reality'. It is true that William Blake described that founding statement of the new empiricism, Bacon's essays, as good advice from Satan's kingdom and announced that Bacon's philosophy had ruined England. No one listened; perhaps quite rightly since both the growth of science and the new conception of man and God, which was to become articulate through Blake and Wordsworth, may have needed the materialistic Deism of the 18th century.

It was not a period of disbelief. Descartes, Boyle and Newton, indeed the most representative minds of the age, were Deists, and affirmed God as a condition of a well-ordered universe and social system. However, their affirmation was by no means of the whole man. They believed in God and they disregarded him. Men gained confidence for their far-ranging exploration of natural phenomena from their conviction that somewhere behind the scenes was a First Cause, remote and benevolent. But – 'presume not God to scan' – since God had no need to meddle with a universe that was ticking over very nicely indeed, man had no business to meddle with God. This attitude enabled the century to get on with its exploration of the 'natural' universe. Despite moments of grandeur, like the closing passage of *The Dunciad*, it made for an exceptional silence as regards visionary poetry.

This silence marks the end of a form of communion between man and God, and the beginning of a new one. Birth depends on some kind of death. Certainly the divorce made by this age between Imagination and Reason, the natural and supernatural worlds seems a condition of the new religious consciousness. The Romantics needed both the revolt against scholastic preconceptions made by their predecessors and their close observation of natural laws. Before the 'Age of Reason' an almost obsessive loyalty to certain 'revealed truths' had inhibited, except for the great and often irascible pioneers of science, a close examination of the natural world. Fire went upward because it was a symbol of the aspiring soul, earth downwards because it was of the same stuff as our perishing bodies; the moon was an image of the deity and in consequence a perfect sphere. Such preconceptions had to go if we were to see the natural world with any clarity. Although they had hardened into dogma they originated from some imaginative or mystical insight rather than the observations of reason. The new science had a deep suspicion of such insight, indeed of any way of knowing other than the exercise of reason, a faculty which they imagined was able to apprehend absolute truth.

After the silence as regards religious poetry of the 18th century, a new dialogue between man and God, the natural and supernatural world is initiated by Blake and Wordsworth. From these poets onwards the greatest religious poetry will depend on imaginative insight and a close observation of man and his environment. A preconception is of little value unless it corresponds to the poets' observation.

However, one must remember Blake's dislike of those 'general truths' so beloved of the Augustans and his conviction that a 'fool sees not the same tree that a wise man sees'. For the new poetry observation far exceeds the scope of an everyday intelligence and those worthy generalizations beloved by Blake's predecessors. Intellect is a useful tool, but real observation depends upon a response of the whole being. In the ultimate book of *The Prelude* which describes the poet's vision on the summit of Snowdon, Wordsworth suggests that this total response exceeds both the finite intelligence and the finite human being. It is linked with the creative power of God, a power which also expresses itself through the phenomena of Nature, in this case the crags and cloud-hidden streams of a mountain.

> The Power which these
> Acknowledge when thus moved, which Nature thus
> Thrusts forth upon the senses, is the express
> Resemblance, in the fulness of its strength
> Made visible, a genuine Counterpart
> And Brother of the glorious faculty
> Which higher minds bear with them as their own.

If Nature is an active expression of the Divine Imagination, if the Divine Imagination is a 'counterpart and brother' of the human imagination, then all knowledge, whether of God or Nature or Man is, in a sense, self-knowledge. Wordsworth and Blake affirm an at-oneness between psychology, theology and natural science. This at-oneness depends upon a working together of imaginative insight and observation. Blake's *A Poison Tree*,[1] for example, is based upon an exceptional understanding of human behaviour. He states, and long before Freud, how destructive it is to deny some human truth, in this case anger. But the human situation in all Blake's poems has a supernatural resonance. So has the world of the animals and

> The Bleat, the Bark, Bellow & Roar
> Are Waves that Beat on Heaven's Shore.[2]

It is the same with Wordsworth. The mystical passages of *The Prelude* are born from some deeply felt and

---

[1] *Songs of Experience.*   [2] *Auguries of Innocence.*

closely observed experience. It is the poet's physical involvement with the rock and heather of a crag, the recovery of a body from a lake, snaring wild birds or ice-skating that make him aware of the supernatural world which overshadows such phenomena. After a temporary absence God is once more immanent within his creation. His mystery cannot be exorcized by a first cause or 'good sense'. It is here within us.

> For I must tread on shadowy ground, must sink
> Deep – and, aloft ascending, breathe in worlds
> To which the heaven of heavens is but a veil.
> All strength – all terror, single or in bands
> That ever was put forth in personal form –
> Jehovah – with his thunder, and the choir
> Of shouting Angels and the empyreal thrones –
> I pass them unalarmed. Not Chaos, not
> The darkest pit of lowest Erebus,
> Nor aught of blinder vacancy, scooped out
> By help of dreams – can breed such fear and awe
> As fall upon us often when we look
> Into our Minds, into the Mind of Man –
> My haunt, and the main region of my song.

That tremendous affirmation from the *Excursion*[1] might serve as a manifesto for the revolution of man's awareness of himself which occurs at the end of the 18th century. This new awareness is still the impetus of our religious poetry, and it has achieved some scientific expression through the work of Freud and Jung and their followers. It is true that Blake said he found Wordsworth's lines so presumptuous that they made him ill. But his indisposition is astonishing when we consider this quatrain from his *Everlasting Gospel*.

[1] Preface to the edition of 1814.

If thou humblest thyself, thou humblest me;
Thou also dwelst in Eternity.
Thou art a Man, God is no more,
Thine own Humanity learn to Adore . . .

'The body', Blake wrote, 'is that portion of the soul discerned by the five senses.' Finite phenomena are the manifestation of a divine or supernatural order of being which can be known by man's imaginative apprehension both of himself and Nature.

Though our ability to apprehend is by no means confined to the intellect it is extremely limited. We are closed within the small circle of a finite ego and only aware of a skin of existence. However, it is possible to enlarge our awareness and so take a fuller part in the dialogue between man and God.

'If the doors of perception were cleansed every thing would appear to man as it is, infinite. For man has closed himself up, till he sees all things thro' narrow chinks of his cavern.'[1] Perception is enlarged if we break out of the cavern or 'mundane shell'. Although this process is similar to the Christian 'death in life', Blake does not express it in traditional Christian terms but creates his own imagery. The new poets are religious in that they are concerned with the inward and spiritual journey of man, and the relationship of man and nature to an order of existence which is not circumscribed by time and space. They are unorthodox because, although their explorations may draw on the Christian revelation, they are by no means circumscribed by its doctrine. For Wordsworth, Blake, Shelley, Yeats and, with some reservations, Browning and Tennyson, Christianity is one way by which some

[1] *The Marriage of Heaven and Hell.*

96

poetic insight may be substantiated, but their work rarely corresponds to orthodox Christianity.

The difference between this new poetry and the religious verse of the 18th century is unmistakable. For the poets of the 18th century the supernatural and numinous were deeply suspect. It is true that they took some form of Christian orthodoxy for granted but unlike their successors, the Romantics and Victorians, religion was not a main theme of their work. An obeisance was made to Christianity which was both correct and distant; only in the hymns of this age do we find good minor devotional verse which is infused with deep feeling.

The religious poetry of the 17th century is orthodox as well, but as I have said already the poets of this age express their deepest convictions and conflicts in Christian terms. The new religious poetry that follows the Augustan Age shares the personal religious conviction that we find in the work of Herbert or Donne but it is not bound by clerical dogma. Indeed Blake – like many thinkers at the turn of the century – felt that the Church had imposed a totally false pattern of behaviour upon the reality of human feelings. Its God was Nobodaddy and its priests far from seeking to bring more abundant life were responsible for the repression of creative energy.

> I went to the Garden of Love,
> And saw what I never had seen:
> A Chapel was built in the midst,
> Where I used to play on the green.
>
> And the gates of this Chapel were shut,
> And 'Thou shalt not' writ over the door;
> So I turn'd to the Garden of Love
> That so many sweet flowers bore;

> And I saw it was filled with graves,
> And tomb-stones where flowers should be;
> And Priests in black gowns were walking their rounds,
> And binding with briars my joys & desires.[1]

In such a poem Blake is not merely concerned like Rousseau with the corruption of an intrinsically good human nature by 'institutions'. He believes the 'lapsed' state of the soul cannot be explained by the attritions of Church or State. But for Blake the Church far from being the way by which we can transcend our 'fallen' humanity, affirms the 'mind forged' manacles of our bondage.

> How the chimney-sweeper's cry
> Every blackening Church appals;
> And the hapless soldier's sigh
> Runs in blood down palace walls.[2]

Blake's work gives the impression that he had exceptional insight into the Christ of the Gospels. He condemned priests because he felt they distorted the Gospels and turned the Christ who said 'I am come that ye may have life and that ye may have it more abundantly' into an enemy of creative energy.

'The wrath of the lion is the wisdom of God', 'The nakedness of woman is the work of God', but 'As the caterpiller chooses the fairest leaves to lay her eggs on, so the priest lays his curse on the fairest joys'. Those *Proverbs of Hell*[3] are not out of harmony with *The Statue and the Bust*, *Two in the Campagna*, indeed many of Browning's poems. They cannot be reconciled with such a 17th century poem as Herbert's address, *The Priesthood*, written before he took holy orders.

[1] *The Garden of Love (Songs of Experience).*
[2] *London, ibid.*   [3] *The Marriage of Heaven and Hell.*

Blest Order, which in power doth so excel,
That with the one hand thou liftest to the sky,
And with the other throwest down to hell
In thy just censures; fain would I draw nigh;
Fain put thee on, exchanging my lay sword
    For that of the Holy Word.

Blake seeks to pass through any orthodox interpretation into some direct communion with Christ.

'Good & Evil are no more!
Sinai's trumpets, cease to roar!
Cease, finger of God, to write!
The Heavens are not clean in thy Sight.

Thou art Good, & thou Alone;
Nor may the sinner cast one stone.
To be Good only, is to be
A God or else a Pharasee.'

He believed that the essence of Christ's teaching was the forgiveness of sin; a belief that might be shared by some theologians. But his interpretation of forgiveness in *The Everlasting Gospel* depends upon his own experience, experience which though it may be enlightened and confirmed by the Gospels has little to do with their latter day interpretations.

My Spectre around me night & day
Like a Wild beast guards my way.

We must accept the shadow side of ourselves, the Spectre, if the Marriage of Heaven and Hell is to take place and man achieve that spiritual and physical wholeness symbolized by Jerusalem. As Blake's 'Tiger' poem suggests it is hard to accept the 'fearful symmetry' of destructive and creative energy. But only

when this Marriage of Heaven and Hell has taken
place can we escape from 'Sinai's Law' and, going beyond the opposites of love and hate, forgive both ourselves and other people.

> Let us agree to give up Love,
> And root up the infernal grove;
> Then shall we return & see
> The worlds of happy Eternity.
>
> & Throughout all Eternity
> I forgive you, you forgive me.
> As our dear Redeemer said:
> 'This the Wine & this the Bread.'

The resolution and serenity of those verses are not
unlike the ending of Yeats's *A Dialogue of Self and
Soul*.

> I am content to follow to its source
> Every event in action or in thought;
> Measure the lot; forgive myself the lot!
> When such as I cast out remorse
> So great a sweetness flows into the breast
> We must laugh and we must sing,
> We are blest by everything,
> Everything we look upon is blest.[1]

The conception of forgiveness in both poems, of a
resolution beyond good and evil comes from the unity
of Psychology and Theology which characterizes religious poetry from Blake onwards. Blake draws on
Christianity but one realizes how little he wrote from
within a central Christian tradition, if one compares
The Everlasting Gospel with Donne's *A Hymn to God*

[1] W. B. Yeats, *The Winding Stair and Other Poems* (1933)
(*The Collected Poems of W. B. Yeats*, 2nd ed., Macmillan, 1950).

the Father. The author is passionately involved with each poem. But Donne's conception of sin and forgiveness is in complete harmony with traditional Christianity. His 'sin of fear' is real enough but the movement of his poem – it is both majestic and tentative – implies a resolution of the fear in terms of the Christianity in which the poem lives and moves.

> Wilt Thou forgive that sin where I begun,
> Which is my sin, though it were done before?
> Wilt Thou forgive that sin, through which I run,
> And do run still: though still I do deplore?
> When Thou hast done, Thou hast not done,
> For, I have more.
>
> I have a sin of fear, that when I have spun
> My last thread, I shall perish on the shore;
> Swear by Thyself, that at my death Thy son
> Shall shine as He shines now, and heretofore;
> And, having done that, Thou hast done,
> I fear no more.[1]

'Thou hast done'; the word play of the penultimate line of the poem is deeply serious. Donne surrenders himself through God's Son, to the paternal God of orthodox Christianity. Despite the turbulence of his life it is difficult not to believe his justly famous hymn celebrates a state of grace and resolution. I say a 'state of grace' rather than 'personal integration' or 'wholeness' because for Donne the knowledge of God is not synonymous with a knowledge of the deeper reaches of the self or Nature. He did realize that 'no man is an island' and that 'any man's death diminisheth me'. But although One Man is Everyman and Everyman

---

[1] John Donne, *Divine Poems* (c. 1610).

may be possessed by God, the distinction between man and God remains. The poet who became Dean of St Paul's would have found little meaning in Blake's,

> Thou art a Man, God is no more,
> Thine own Humanity, learn to Adore.[1]

As a result of his experience on Grasmere in a stolen boat, Wordsworth says,

>   . . . my brain
> Worked with a dim and undetermined sense
> Of unknown modes of being . . . . .
> . . . . call it solitude
> Or blank desertion. No familiar shapes
> Remained, no pleasant images of trees,
> Of sea or sky, no colours of green fields;
> But huge and mighty forms, that do not live
> Like living men, moved slowly through the mind
> By day, and were a trouble to my dreams.[2]

That immediate but, as far as any orthodox belief goes, quite untrammelled experience of the supernatural world, bears little or no relationship to Donne's communion with a personal God to whom he pleads,

> Swear by Thyself, that at my death, Thy son
> Shall shine as He shines now, and heretofore . . .

In the 17th century religious poetry was determined by Christian doctrine. Donne and Herbert were not concerned with 'a presence far more deeply interfused' or that 'Jerusalem' in which Blake saw a revolution of conflicting energies which were both human and divine. Their desire was for a communion with a paternal God through the medium of His Son, Jesus Christ.

[1] *The Everlasting Gospel.*   [2] *The Prelude.*

Christianity is not a parochial religion. Donne could breathe freely within it and write poems which are not limited by Christian dogma.

> Seal then this bill of my Divorce to All,
> On whom those fainter beams of love did fall;
> Marry those loves, which in youth scattered be
> On Fame, Wit, Hopes (false mistresses) to Thee.
> Churches are best for Prayer, that have least light:
> To see God only, I go out of sight:
>   And to 'scape stormy days, I choose
>   An Everlasting night.[1]

Those lines affirm a desire to be liberated from temporal attachments which is shared by all the great religions of the world. But the verse is governed by a Christian intention. Wordsworth's *Immortality Ode* is a religious poem which can be associated with no one religion. It celebrates the 'religious instinct', but the 'obstinate questionings' by that instinct of 'sense and outward things' implies a questioning of all data, including those of the Christian religion.

> Not for these I raise
> The song of thanks and praise;
> But for those obstinate questionings
> Of sense and outward things,
> Fallings from us, vanishings;
> Blank misgivings of a Creature
> Moving about in worlds not realised,
> High instincts before which our mortal Nature
> Did tremble like a guilty thing surprised . . .

Wordsworth tells us that as a young man he had often to clutch at some material object to recall himself from

[1] Donne, *A Hymn to Christ, at the Authors Last Going into Germany* (*Divine Poems*).

'an abyss of idealism'. His own mystical experience assured him of the reality of the spiritual world, and in his great religious poetry, *Tintern Abbey*, for instance, or *The Prelude*, he tries to keep as close as words will allow to what he has experienced of 'unknown modes of being'. It is significant that in the poetry of his 'great period' he seldom uses the word 'God'. Because of its time honoured associations that word would blur the immediate apprehension of the supernatural that he tries to communicate. Jung has pointed out how great may be the strain if we attempt to confront the supernatural directly without the medium of traditional religious symbols. Blake did maintain such a naked confrontation throughout a long life, but the friendly intimacy between this poet and the divine realm is as exceptional as his personal sanctity. After many years of direct religious experience, Wordsworth found the strain too much and turned to the orthodox Christianity of his Ecclesiastical Sonnets. Despite their technical skill these poems are lifeless because they are written in a religious tradition which could no longer sustain visionary poetry.

Although the essence of Wordsworth was not always appreciated or understood in the 19th century, and the work of Blake was not assimilated by a great poet until our own age and W. B. Yeats, from the end of the 18th century onwards, the direction of religious poetry in England is that first taken by Blake and Wordsworth. The new attitude is exploratory. Its poets may draw with reverence and conviction upon Christianity but, at their best, are not circumscribed by Christian doctrine. At times both Tennyson and Browning, the great Victorian successors of the Romantics, attempt to

write verse in an orthodox Christian tradition and pro-
test a 'simple faith' which they did not possess. Their
response to the supernatural is often both sincere and
tentative. But far from being 'delivered by the Holy
Ghost from a multitude of opinions', when their response is most strenuous it includes a number of
opinions, whose conflict cannot be solved in Christian
terms. Indeed the particular significance of such poems
as *Cleon*, *Karshish* and *In Memoriam* itself comes from
the way these poems express with telling accuracy a
number of conflicting ideas whose tensions they sustain but do not attempt to resolve. It is in the Victorian age that the uncertainty of the father of the
possessed child – 'Lord, I believe, help thou my unbe-
lief' – begins to achieve a religious sincerity which
may exceed that of unquestioning belief. Though
Tennyson may question the existence of a supernatural power or the benevolent intention of God towards his creation, he will affirm God also. It is the
counterpoint of doubt and affirmation which give to
his religious work an especial poignancy. When asked
in later years whether he was a Christian, Browning
responded with a resounding 'No'. Perhaps his response was not unconnected with those members of the
'Browning Society', satirized by Max Beerbohm. But
although his poetry never questions the existence of a
supernatural world, such works as *The Heretic's
Tragedy* and *The Ring and the Book* do express, and
with great power, the difficulty of making any finite
reconciliation between the conception of a benevolent
God and the reality of human evil. Moreover, in other
great religious poems, *Cleon*, for instance, and *Karshish*, although he makes an oblique examination of

Christianity and its interpretation of existence, he does not commit himself to such an interpretation. His best poems leave the question open. As he is a poet of the Victorian – and our own age – this is the most strenuous response; a direct and simple answer would belittle the question.

Unfortunately, in the minor verse of Tennyson and Browning the religious question is both begged and belittled by an answer which may be appropriate to the popular sentiment of their age but bears scant relevance to their poetic imagination. There are many reasons for this, and they are related to the ability of these poets to make significant religious verse of doubt and faith, affirmation and denial. When they sustained the tension between those not unrelated opposites they wrote well. When they write of a solution to these conflicts, which they have not reached, which given the 'climate of their age' it was not possible for them to reach, then their religious verse is false and without interest.

Tennyson and Browning can write religious poetry which may be of constant significance. They also write sentimental religious banalities and, in the case of Browning, doggerel verse sermons which are didactic and profoundly dull. This is one aspect of the tendency of these poets to produce very good and bad work. I have suggested some general reasons for this variability in a previous chapter, but must examine it more fully in relationship to their religious work.

Blake wrote of one of his poems, 'I may indeed praise it for I am only the secretary, the author is in Heaven'. He did not intend this as dramatic hyperbole but as an appraisal of the communion between himself and the invisible world. It is this communion which gives him the confidence to write with exceptional honesty. On the other hand when attempting to unravel the complex symbolism of the Prophetic Books one may well regret that he had no relationship with an appreciative public whose comments might have made his work more accessible to the reader.

The attitude of the 'general' reader to Wordsworth is suggested by Byron –

> And Wordsworth, in a rather long 'Excur-
> sion'
> (I think the quarto holds five hundred
> pages),
> Has given a sample from the vasty version
> Of his new system to perplex the sages;
> 'Tis poetry – at least by his assertion,
> And may appear so when the dog-star
> rages –
> And he who understands it would be able
> To add a story to the Tower of Babel.[1]

However, despite Byron's irony, Wordsworth was supported by a few people who could understand his greatest work and – in the case of Coleridge – criticized a falling off from his high vision. But there were only a few people. A reason why the first generation of Romantics could express their vision with such fidelity was their freedom from any pressure by a large reading public to accommodate their work to platitude and convention. Not that their freedom from such pressure reduced their sense of being dedicated bards, and with a mission to the public. Wordsworth's ostensible object in writing *The Prelude* was to examine the personal

[1] Lord Byron, *Dedication*, IV (*Don Juan*).

development which fitted him for his high calling. In his address to the Christians, from *Jerusalem*, Blake writes 'Let every Christian, as much as in him lies, engage himself openly and publicly before all the world in some mental pursuit for the building of the new Jerusalem.' His sense of commitment is obvious. But both for Blake and the earlier Wordsworth the sense of mission was very largely dependent on their poetic vision. I do not suggest that either Tennyson or Browning were lacking in visionary power. They are major poets. Consequently though the intellect of these men is an ingredient of their greatest poetry, such poetry in its scope of thought and feeling seems to exceed their everyday capacities. But it does seem that the Victorian poets were more subject to the pressures of public opinion than their predecessors. Jung calls that element of the human psyche which is not born out of the growing pains of experience but has merely taken over and identified itself with certain current attitudes of thought and feeling, the Persona. It is not so much the intellect but this Persona which is more dominant in the work of Tennyson and Browning than that of Blake and the young Wordsworth.

Auden writes of people in general, 'unluckily they were their situation'. It is not possible to separate anyone from the age he lives in; Browning and Tennyson were particularly susceptible to public opinion because the Victorian literary public, if not as single minded as that of the 18th century, was larger and more powerful and homogenous than at the time of the first Romantics. What is more they bought poetry not only in large quantities but, at times, with real judgment. The success of *Lalla Rookh* and *Summoned by Bells* is not remarkable. But it is both remarkable and to the credit of the age that *In Memoriam* was an immediate best seller. Browning only 'hit the market' in the latter part of his life, but his wife's work went into edition after edition, and so did the poems of Tennyson. It was always possible the Victorian poets might get a backing for their arduous vocation, not in terms of some visionary assurance or a small but appreciative circle but hard cash and a large vociferous audience. After all, though Wordsworth was dubious whether he had made £1,000 for his entire life's work, Moore made several thousands from *Lalla Rookh* alone.

Unfortunately, though *In Memoriam* was extremely popular the public had an equal relish for Tennyson's sentimental and didactic verse. The poet's wife was a piece of human litmus paper. He had only to dip the devoted creature into some new poem and her change of colour would suggest its value – in current market prices, not unfortunately in terms of poetry. *In Memoriam* was written through years of bitter solitude and neglect, but even at the height of his fame Tennyson's gifts were only in part diverted by popular acclaim and he continued to write significant poetry. But the temptation was always there, and from time to time both Tennyson and Browning succumbed to it. One could, at the risk of failure, self doubt and anxiety, write what one really knew and felt in those moments of heightened awareness which are the poetic *raison d'être*. One could, when imagination was at a low ebb, get a copy of verses under way by a desire for acclaim as little related to poetry as is the sermon of a popular preacher to God. Such verse flatters the public. It substitutes the Persona for the critical intellect and exchanges 'what I feel and know' for 'what I feel the "best people" feel they ought to feel and what I know the "best people" know they ought to know'.

Tennyson and Browning hover between such truth and falsity and the dichotomy is most apparent in their religious poetry. Such work is moving, sincere and close to some essence of the divided Victorian Age and our own, when its religious statements are both tentative and uncommitted. Perhaps it is just this lack of commitment which is the particular addition of these poets to the spiritual affirmations of Blake and Wordsworth. Blake's couplet —

> If the sun and moon should doubt
> They'd immediately go out[1]

gains a further resonance when juxtaposed with these lines from Tennyson's *In Memoriam*:

> Behold, we know not anything;
>> I can but trust that good shall fall
>> At last — far off — at last, to all,
> And every winter turn to spring.
>
> So runs my dream: but what am I?
>> An infant crying in the night:
>> An infant crying for the light:
> And with no language but a cry.

That is the despair of a man confronting a human nature and a material universe which are given meaning neither by revealed religion nor mystical insight. Moreover Tennyson does not share the certainty of the 18th century that an examination of natural laws by Science will reveal the benevolent intentions of a God who cares

---

[1] *Auguries of Innocence.*

110

for his creation. At times he will by-pass his doubt; *In Memoriam* ends with the statement that man is evolving into some Thurberesque entity called 'a noble type', and existence presided over by a well-meaning Deity,

> No longer half-akin to brute,
>   For all we thought and loved and did,
>   And hoped, and suffered, is but seed
> Of what in them is flower and fruit;
>
> Whereof the man, that with me trod
>   This planet, was a noble type
>   Appearing ere the time was ripe,
> That friend of mine who lives in God . . .

'Them' in the fourth line refers to some future generation who will be the 'flower and fruit' of the imperfect but suffering humanity of preceding ages. These supermen and women are anticipated by Hallam. Tennyson like most Victorians was worried by the seeming contradictions between Christianity and Science. I say 'seeming contradictions' because from our present standpoint there may appear to be no intrinsic opposition between Christianity and Science, only between their simplifications by the Victorian mind. The final passage of *In Memoriam* rings false because Tennyson is writing of a resolution between Science and Christianity, doubt and faith which he had not attained in his inner life. Given 'the climate of thought' of this age such a resolution, even if achieved in a poet's life, could not be expressed directly and in cerebral terms; only by such a magnificent but oblique image as Rossetti's *The Woodspurge* –

> From perfect grief there need not be
> Wisdom or even memory:

111

> One thing then learnt remains to me, –
> The woodspurge has a cup of three.

It would be inept to suggest that the three-fold cup of *The Woodspurge* can be fixed down to anything but itself, let alone the Trinity or a union between sensual experience, mystical insight and empirical observation! But the final image of Rossetti's poem does achieve a sense of quiet resolution, whereas the concluding passage of *In Memoriam* offers us only opinion. Highly debatable at that. Attempting to harmonize the contemporary idea of Evolution with Christianity, Tennyson slurs over the Christian belief in personal salvation and the intrinsic value of each human soul. By suggesting that individual hope and suffering in a present moment is of no personal value but seed which will bear fruit in a distant future the poet anticipates the theory of Nietsche and Bernard Shaw that men and women are not ends in themselves but means to the 'Übermensch'. Since the whole tenour of *In Memoriam* denies such a conception and asserts, often with extreme poignancy, and in the teeth of apparent evidence, that the individual is the standard of all values and circumscribed neither by space and time, one realizes that in the conclusion of this poem Tennyson substitutes superficial opinion for personal conviction.

Eliot has written with considerable justification that *In Memoriam* is a great religious poem but a poem of religious doubt. Certainly Tennyson's superbly formulated despair, as he questions a universe whose amorality and lack of meaning seems to be substantiated by Natural science, is far nearer to religious affirmation

than Addison's hymn about those inane heavenly
bodies —

> Forever singing as they shine,
> 'The hand that made us is divine.'

'Nature' which seemed in the 18th century to be
irrefutable evidence for Divine good sense and benevolence appears under the first impact of the theory of
Evolution to be both indifferent and amoral. Men and
women are mere incidents of this impersonal process.
It is the conflict between Tennyson's conviction of personal immortality and his fear that this conviction is
contradicted by Science that creates the especial tension of *In Memoriam.*

> 'So careful of the type?' but no.
>   From scarped cliff and quarried stone
>   She cries 'A thousand types are gone:
> I care for nothing, all shall go.
>
> 'Thou makest thine appeal to me:
>   I bring to life, I bring to death:
>   The spirit does but mean the breath:
> I know no more.' And he, shall he,
>
> Man, her last work, who seem'd so fair,
>   Such splendid purpose in his eyes,
>   Who roll'd the psalm to wintry skies,
> Who built him fanes of fruitless prayer,
>
> Who trusted God was love indeed
>   And love Creation's final law —
>   Tho' Nature, red in tooth and claw
> With ravine, shriek'd against his creed —
>
> Who loved, who suffer'd countless ills,
>   Who battled for the True, the Just,

Be blown about the desert dust,
Or seal'd within the iron hills?

No doubt that question can only be answered by such
an affirmation of faith born out of mystical experience
as we find in Blake's *Auguries of Innocence*.

The Bleat, the Bark, Bellow & Roar
Are Waves that Beat on Heaven's Shore.
The Babe that weeps the Rod beneath
Writes Revenge in realms of death.
The Beggar's Rags, fluttering in Air,
Does to Rags the Heavens tear.
The Soldier arm'd with Sword & Gun,
Palsied strikes the Summer's Sun.

Blake believed that creation is related to eternity,
that all living creatures have a significance beyond
their 'Vegetable Universe'. Imaginatively, I believe
that Tennyson had a similar faith, but it was not supported by his critical intellect which in common with
some of the most acute minds of his age, felt with considerable dread that the new scientific discoveries contradicted the experience of religion. In his greatest
poetry Tennyson encompasses both his imaginative
faith and his intellectual doubt. Many passages of *In
Memoriam* do express doubt, but with such extreme
poignancy and power that the emotional tenour of the
verses contradict their intellectual uncertainty, and may
seem, paradoxically, to make a religious affirmation.

Unfortunately, Tennyson does not always sustain
the rhapsodic anxious questioning of his finest poetry.
Partly from a desire to gain certainty and resolve the
tension between doubt and faith, partly from a desire
to give his public what it wanted (the reasons are not

dissimilar), he tries to answer those questions which – given the poet he was – are themselves their most adequate answer.

> That God, who ever lives and loves,
>> One God, one law, one element,
>> And one far-off divine event,
> To which the whole creation moves.

In that final verse of *In Memoriam*, as in the stanzas which he placed at the beginning of the poem and which are included in our hymn books, Tennyson attempts to resolve in traditional Christian terms the tension between doubt and faith which gives his poem its sustained energy. His imagination does not seem deeply involved with 'That God, who ever lives and loves' or 'one far-off divine event, to which the whole creation moves'. By this – as far as poetry goes – outmoded rhetoric he is seeking to fob off his anxious uncertainty and, with one eye on the box-office, make a bow to popular opinion. Such opinion since he was a poet of great sensibility and intelligence was not really his own. If his poetry had not made us aware of this sensibility then the first and last stanzas of *In Memoriam* might not be a falsification of talent. They would be on a par with those hymns of the 18th and 19th centuries which retain their appeal and are the work of a faith to which the term 'simple' may be applied with no derogatory significance. But it is not the faith of a Wesley, an Isaac Watts or a Bishop Heber that we find in Tennyson's masterpiece but the tension of doubt and faith, and a realization of how great is our dereliction if life has no spiritual significance.

I falter where I firmly trod,
    And falling with my weight of cares
    Upon the great worlds altar stairs
That slope thro' darkness up to God,

I stretch lame hands of faith, and grope,
    And gather dust and chaff, and call
    To what I feel is Lord of all
And faintly trust the larger hope.

Chapter Four

Browning's Religious Poetry

I

Through such souls alone
God stooping shows sufficient of His light
For us i' the dark to rise by.
Pompilia (end of Bk VII,
The Ring and the Book).[1]

In the poetry of Robert Browning, we do not find that
insoluble conflict between imagination and reason, the
'felt' truths of religion and the intellectual truths of
Victorian science that characterizes so much of Tennyson's work. It is not a denigration of Tennyson's
achievement to suggest that the present attitude to
science and religion has considerably modified if not re-
solved their conflict. But I do suggest that the ability of
Browning's best religious poetry to reconcile – it is an
arduous and at times long-winded process – imaginative insight and intellectual exploration, should be
sympathetic to our own day and age. His great religious poems depend upon an enquiring intelligence,
which although it is allied from time to time with
mystical insight, takes the same passionate but detached

[1] 4 vols (Smith, Elder, 1868–9); Vol. II of 2-vol. collection
(*ibid.*, 1896); reissued (John Murray, 1919, reprinted 1951).

interest in the supernatural that one finds in the writing of Jung, Maurice Nicoll, Teilhard de Chardin, Aldous Huxley and, with some reservations, Ouspensky.

However, Tennyson did not sustain the tension of his great religious verse, and Browning is his contemporary. At times this poet will substitute garrulous and uninspired religiosity for his acute examination – unlike Tennyson he can relish its uncertainty – of the rapport between a natural and supernatural world. Not only that, at times Browning will throw subtlety, intellect and insight to the winds and fall back on the rant of a mediocre dissenting pulpit. In fact his religious poetry is hedged about with thickets of very bad verse indeed, and to reach it one must clear away a great deal of doggerel.

That the rollicking jingoism of *Saul*[1] has been so popular only attests the coarse palate of Browning's anthologists, and that anthologies are based upon other anthologies.

I believe it! 'tis Thou, God, that givest, 'tis I who receive:
In the first is the last, in thy will is my power to believe.
All's one gift: thou canst grant it moreover, as prompt to
    my prayer
As I breathe out this breath, as I open these arms to the
   air . . .

As is always the case when Browning is writing from public opinion, from his social 'persona' rather than his muse, in that passage there is a correspondence between the obviousness of the rhymes and rhythms and the platitudes of thought.

Another anthology piece, *Rabbi Ben Ezra*,[2] al-

---

[1] *Men and Women.*   [2] *Dramatis Personae.*

though its thought is of a greater depth and subtlety than *Saul*, lacks that tentativeness, which I suggest is an essential condition of good religious poetry of present-day significance. It never rises beyond the level of an intelligent but uninspired sermon.

> Fool! All that is, at all,
> Lasts ever, past recall;
> Earth changes, but thy soul and God stand sure:
> What entered into thee,
> *That* was, is, and shall be:
> Time's wheel runs back or stops; Potter and clay
> endure.

Some of the thought of that passage may be implied in Wordsworth's *Immortality Ode*, but in the Ode statements about the supernatural are acceptable because they suggest possibilities but make no definite conclusion. We accept them because they say 'This may be' rather than 'This is', 'this may be possible' rather than 'this I know for a fact'. One rejects Browning's bombastic assault because he is treating of the supernatural in terms more appropriate to a guide book to Brighton or the mechanism of the internal combustion engine.

Perhaps *Christmas-Eve*[1] is the most interesting example of Browning's bad religious verse. It describes the poet's visit to a number of religious celebrations including Mass at St Peter's, Rome, a lecture on humanistic ethics by a German professor and a service in a Dissenting Chapel; that kind of service which Browning and his father attended as a sop, if not to Cerberus, to the poet's mother who was an ardent Dissenter. The

---

[1] *Christmas-Eve and Easter-Day* (1850).

poem says that provided it is genuine the Almighty derives satisfaction from the most crude and simple expression of love.

> God who registers the cup
> Of mere cold water, for His sake
> To a disciple rendered up,
> Disdains not His own thirst to slake
> At the poorest love was ever offered . . .

The interest of that paraphrase of the Gospel's 'If ye have done it unto the least of these little ones ye have done it unto me' lies in the extreme efficiency with which it deprives Christ's statement of its immense suggestiveness and power and converts it into a 'great thought' for the 'Wayside Pulpit'.

Christmas-Eve is both a very interesting and a very bad poem. Only in its passages of satirical portraiture is Browning's imagination involved. In the bulk of the poem he is turning into doggerel verse certain platitudes of Victorian religious opinion, more particularly the homely and pious truisms of Dissent which he learnt at his mother's knee; truisms which are totally incompatible with his own personal concern with morality and the supernatural.

> Earth breaks up, time drops away,
> In flows heaven, with its new day
> Of endless life, when He who trod,
> Very Man and very God,
> This earth in weakness, shame and pain,
> Dying the death whose signs remain
> Up yonder on the accursed tree, —
> Shall come again, no more to be
> Of captivity the thrall,

> But the one God, all in all,
> King of kings, and Lord of lords,
> As His servant John received the words,
> 'I died, and live for evermore!'

This is by no means the language of poetry, it is sermonizing in verse, and at a fairly low level. Browning
makes no effort to find words that will create in the
minds of his readers an impression of the return of
Christ. Nor does he suggest, as Blake does in the famous
song from *Jerusalem*, that the return can be a perennial experience within the human psyche.

> Bring me my Bow of burning gold:
> Bring me my Arrows of desire . . .
>
> I will not cease from Mental Fight,
> Nor shall my Sword sleep in my hand
> Till we have built Jerusalem
> In England's green and pleasant land.

The point there is the 'mental fight', and the serene
strength with which Blake expresses that sense of
beatitude and resolution which he names *Jerusalem*.
Blake's poem comes out of a deeply felt experience
whereas Browning's comes out of a shallow, one might
say 'time serving', response to a banal version of Christian orthodoxy which bears little or no relationship to
his deeper intuitions and convictions about the life of
the spirit. But the climax of the poem's falsity is not
such a threadbare poetical phrase as 'Very Man and
very God' or 'King of kings and Lord of lords'. It is
the poet's supposed vision of Christ; a vision described
in terms which would delight the heart of any pro-
ducer of a super-technicolor film about Jesus; and was

probably no more a part of the poet's actual experience than the ascent of Everest.

> All at once I looked up with terror.
> He was there.
> He Himself with His human air,
> On the narrow pathway, just before:
> I saw the back of Him, no more –
> He had left the chapel, then, as I.
> I forgot all about the sky.
> No face: only the sight
> Of a sweepy Garment, vast and white,
> With a hem that I could recognise.

However, a few lines later Browning does see the Son of God directly and is taken by Christ on a personally conducted tour of various religious or quasi-religious institutions. First to Rome; and Catholicism does not come off at all well, though we are told there is a grain of truth – even in Popery.

> Though Rome's gross yoke
> Drops off, no more to be endured,
> Her teaching is not so obscured
> By errors and perversities,
> That no truth.shines athwart the lies . . .

It is worth noting that when Browning is writing from opinion rather than knowledge, from what other people feel and think rather than from what he himself thinks and feels, it is then that his perverse rhyming phobia – it depends on 'cleverness' – takes over. In this poem we have such weird conjunctions as 'artist' and 'departest', 'life-size' and 'wife's eyes', 'bigger' and 'figure'.

The poem ends on a lighter note with the poet

stating that for himself Wesleyan Dissent is, despite a certain crudeness, the most satisfactory form of Christianity. A conclusion which can be reconciled neither with the great religious poetry of Browning nor the three thunderous 'No's' which were his reply in later life to the question whether he was an orthodox Christian.

> And let us hope
> That no worse blessing befal the Pope,
> Turn'd sick at last of the day's buffoonery,
> Of his posturings and his petticoatings,
> Beside the Bourbon bully's gloatings
> In the bloody orgies of drunk poltroonery!
> Nor may the Professor forego its peace
> At Göttingen, presently, when, in the dusk
> Of his life, if his cough, as I fear, should increase,
> Prophesied of by that horrible husk;
> And when, thicker and thicker, the darkness fills
> The world through his misty spectacles,
> And he gropes for something more substantial
> Than a fable, myth, or personification,
> May Christ do for him, what no mere man shall,
> And stand confessed as the God of salvation!
> Meantime, in the still recurring fear
> Lest myself, at unawares, be found,
> While attacking the choice of my neighbours round,
> Without my own made – I choose here!
>
> I put up pencil and join chorus
> To Hepzibah Tune, without further apology,
> The last five verses of the third section
> Of the seventeenth hymn in Whitfield's Collection . . .

The ending of this unsatisfactory poem is ironical. It is significant that all the best passages of *Christmas-Eve*

123

share this irony. In the description of the congregation in the Wesleyan chapel there is a savage Dickensian zest.

> But the flock sate on, divinely flustered,
> Sniffing, methought, its dew of Hermon
> With such content in every snuffle,
> As the devil inside us loves to ruffle.
> My old fat woman purred with pleasure,
> And thumb round thumb went twirling faster,
> While she, to his periods keeping measure,
> Maternally devoured the pastor.
> The man with the handkerchief, untied it,
> Showed us a horrible wen inside it,
> Gave his eyelids yet another screwing,
> And rocked himself as the woman was doing.

As is always the case in Browning's religious as opposed to his love poetry, he is more successful when he writes indirectly through a persona. *A Death in the Desert*[1] is about St John the Evangelist, the last man, the poem suggests, who saw Jesus alive. The saint is dying and his friends and disciples have taken refuge in a desert cave from those who are hounding down the followers of Christ. As usual Browning makes the period and atmosphere in his monologue vivid and alive.

> Beyond, and half way up the mouth o' the cave,
> The Bactrian convert, having his desire,
> Kept watch, and made pretence to graze a goat
> That gave us milk, on rags of various herb,
> Plantain and quitch, the rocks' shade keeps alive:
> So that if any thief or soldier passed,
> (Because the persecution was aware)

[1] *Dramatis Personae.*

124

> Yielding the goat up promptly with his life,
> Such man might pass on, joyful at a prize,
> Nor care to pry into the cool o' the cave.
> Outside was all noon and the burning blue.

In this work and *The Ring and the Book* Browning combines his exploratory interest in the supernatural — an interest which is both psychological and theological — with a more specific concern with Christianity than his other great religious poems, *Karshish*, *Cleon* and *Caliban upon Setebos*.

The dying John comes back to a last but blazing moment of life, not through the wine that is applied to his lips or the ball of perfume that is broken under his nostrils, but because a boy speaks an electrifying phrase of Christ.

> Then the Boy sprang up from his knees, and ran,
> Stung by the splendour of a sudden thought,
> And fetched the seventh plate of graven lead
>
> . . . .
>
> And spoke, as 'twere his mouth proclaiming first,
> 'I am the Resurrection and the Life.'

The saint wakes and starts to speak. Since Browning is deeply involved with his theme what he says is neither platitude nor opinion but a deep and subtle exploration of the supernatural world. The saint is at the point of death and Browning creates the sense of his hovering for a few instants on this dark threshold:

> Yet now I wake in such decrepitude
> As I had slidden down and fallen afar,
> Past even the presence of my former self,
> Grasping the while for stay at facts which snap,
> Till I am found away from my own world,

> Feeling for foot-hold through a blank profound,
> Along with unborn people in strange lands,
> Who say – I hear said or conceive they say –
> 'Was John at all, and did he say he saw?
> Assure us, ere we ask what he might see!'

John wishes to give some assurance of the Christian revelation to others but knows both that he is ceasing to be human and that humanity because of its deep and inevitable involvement in the material world cannot make any complete acceptance of those truths he wishes to affirm.

> And how shall I assure them? Can they share
> – They, who have flesh, a veil of youth and strength
> About each spirit, that needs must bide its time,
> Living and learning still as years assist
> Which wear the thickness thin, and let man see –
> With me who hardly am withheld at all,
> But shudderingly, scarce a shred between,
> Lie bare to the universal prick of light?

'Which wear the thickness thin and let man see.' Here he anticipates the famous lines from Yeats's *Sailing to Byzantium*.[1]

> Soul clap its hands and sing, and louder sing
> For every tatter in its mortal dress . . .

One should also note the last two lines of that quotation from *A Death in the Desert*; an effective reply surely to those myopic critics who say that Browning's poetry lacks the memorable and electrifying phrase. Perhaps the especial interest of this poem today is Browning's

[1] *The Tower* (1928) (*The Collected Poems of W. B. Yeats*, op. cit.).

creation of a man poised between life and death. John
is near the infinity of death. This makes him realize
that men and women rooted in time and materiality
must find it almost impossible to understand infinite
truths. The exposition of Christianity through the
dying John is also of value. One agrees, for instance,
with this passage about 'love' while admitting it has
little poetic resonance.

> For life, with all it yields of joy and woe,
> And hope and fear, – believe the aged friend, –
> Is just our chance o' the prize of learning love . . .

Despite its excessive length, 21,000 lines, and despite
long dreary passages of intellectual gymnastics without
inspiration or interest, *The Ring and the Book*, published in twelve parts between 1868 and 1869, is probably a masterpiece. No doubt every reader must be
his own anthologist of this work. I myself would say
that Book I,[1] Pompilia's death-bed story of her life
(Book VII), the summing up by the Pope (Book X),
and Guido's final self-revelation on the eve of his exe-
cution (Book XI), are of the greatest importance.

The poem fulfils its immense ambitions. Like
Shakespeare's *Macbeth* it tries to comprehend those
unwritten spiritual laws which though they are unen-
forceable by 'the Law' do direct and condition our
lives. It shows the relevance of loss and suffering which
from a purely temporal standard appear intolerable, to
a non-temporal dimension. It is also a most searching
examination of the nature of evil and it achieves these
tasks with a very close correspondence to the Christian
conceptions of sin and redemption.

[1] Title poem.

The poem is in twelve books and it tells the story of the murder by Count Guido Franceschini, a 16th-century Italian nobleman, of his wife Pompilia. In Book I which contains the poet's superb *Invocation* to his dead wife, Browning describes the sources of his information. In Book XII he winds up the threads. The intervening books tell the story twelve times over, each time from a different point of view. This method, though longwinded, gives an impression both of truth's infinite complexity and a man's ability to struggle with great effort through this complexity to some partial understanding of 'reality'. In Book II we have the gossip of half Rome favourable to Guido. In Book III the more judicious half favouring Pompilia. Then we have the analysis of Tertium Quid, a sensitive nobleman. Next we have the speech of Guido in his own defence and here Browning stresses that evil and ignorance work hand in glove. This is followed by the evidence of Giuseppe Caponsacchi, the soldier saint who has attempted to rescue Pompilia from the intolerable persecution of her sinister husband. Then we have Pompilia's death-bed story of her own life (a superb passage), the boring arguments of the Defence and Prosecution, the summing up by the old Pope to whom Guido has appealed and finally Guido's self-revelation.

I mention in a later chapter the poem's unflinching examination of evil. Guido, an ageing parasitic nobleman, marries the young Pompilia because he believes her parents are wealthy and wishes to repair his fortune. When he finds out she is not only poor but the illegitimate daughter of a prostitute, adopted out of kindness by her step-parents, he systematically persecutes his young wife. This persecution is prompted both by his own psychological if not physical impotence – he is incapable of either love or affection – and his desire to drive his wife into infidelity so that he may discard her. There is also the deep antipathy of his tortuous and perverse mind towards the grace and simplicity of his young wife. With the help of the priest, Caponsacchi, Pompilia runs away, gives her child into the care of a peasant family and takes refuge with her parents. Guido tracks her down, murders her parents and with his 'accomplices' fatally wounds his wife. The wounds are all delivered on the face, a traditional revenge on adulterous wives; for although Guido has himself forged letters purporting to be offers of love by the priest, when his wife actually does escape with Caponsacchi he manages to think of himself as an aggrieved husband whose ferocity is justified.

In many sections of the poem Browning is writing with ingenuity but little inspiration and one does get bogged down in thickets of boring verbiage. But for all that *The Ring and the Book* is one of the most profound examinations of the polarities of good and evil in any language. Here is Browning's account of Guido's accomplices, four farm labourers.

(As if he but proposed 'One vineyard more
To dig, ere frost come, then relax indeed!')
'Anywhere, anyhow, anywhy,
Murder me some three people, old and young,
Ye never heard the names of, – and be paid
So much!' And the whole four accede at once.
Demur? Do cattle bidden march or halt?
Is it some lingering habit, old fond faith
I' the lord o' the land, instructs them, – birthright badge

> Of feudal tenure claims its slaves again?
> Not so at all, thou noble human heart!
> All is done purely for the pay, — which, earned,
> And not forthcoming at the instant, makes
> Religion heresy, and the lord o' the land
> Fit subject for a murder in his turn.
> The patron with cut throat and rifled purse,
> Desposited i' the roadside-ditch, his due,
> Nought hinders each good fellow trudging home,
> The heavier by a piece or two in poke,
> And so with new zest to the common life,
> Mattock and spade, plough-tail and waggon-shaft,
> Till some such other piece of luck betide . . .[1]

The post-Hitler generation should understand the
accuracy of that diagnosis of so-called 'simplicity'; a
diagnosis which is utterly incompatible with the myth
of Browning's 'facile optimism'. Few poets make such
a searching examination of the darker side of human
nature.

The Pope's soliloquy contains not only a diagnosis
of the varieties of evil but some of Browning's most
penetrating religious thought. And here the religious
utterance, though Christian, suggests that union of
Theology, Psychology and Natural Science which has
characterized religious thought since Blake and Wordsworth. Pompilia shelters her child from the rapacity of
her husband and the Pope comments:

> Thou at first prompting of what I call God,
> And fools call Nature, didst hear, comprehend,
> Accept the obligation laid on thee,
> Mother Elect, to save the unborn child,
> As brute and bird do, reptile and the fly,

[1] *The Pope* (Bk X).

Ay and, I nothing doubt, even tree, shrub, plant
And flower o' the field, all in a common pact
To worthily defend the trust of trusts,
Life from the Ever Living . . .[1]

It is significant that when Browning is writing, as in many passages of *The Ring and the Book*, with the fullness of his genius we do not have the irritating gibes at Catholicism which disfigure *Christmas-Eve*. The aged Pope is treated with sympathy and deep understanding, both as a man and the Vicar of Christ.

In God's name! Once more on this earth of God's,
While twilight lasts and time wherein to work,
I take His staff with my uncertain hand,
And stay my six and fourscore years, my due
Labour and sorrow, on His judgement-seat,
And forthwith think, speak, act, in place of Him –
The Pope for Christ. Once more appeal is made
From man's assize to mine: I sit and see
Another poor weak trembling human wretch
Pushed by his fellows, who pretend the right,
Up to the gulf which, where I gaze, begins
From this world to the next, – gives way and way,
Just on the edge over the awful dark:
With nothing to arrest him but my feet.[2]

Near to death himself, in those lines and many other passages of the poem the Pope expresses a profound apprehension of the mystery and significance of dying. Finally he condemns Guido to death but to reach this decision he journeys through the wisdom of a lifetime of thought and suffering. This meditation is one

[1] *Ibid.*   [2] *Ibid.*

of the greatest of all Browning's monologues. Literature contains considerably more studies of disintegra-
tion, ignorance and chaos than resolution, because the
former is a more common condition of humanity. But
with this pope Browning brings alive the thought of a
man who has worked out his own salvation. He realizes
his own fallibility both as a man and a pope. Indeed his
meditation starts with a sordid account of papal fallibility – but he also knows that in the temporal world
one must act as best one can with one's limited knowledge.

> Mankind is ignorant, a man am I:
> Call ignorance my sorrow, not my sin!
> So and not otherwise, in after-time,
> If some acuter wit, fresh probing, sound
> This multifarious mass of words and deeds
> Deeper, and reach through guilt to innocence,
> I shall face Guido's ghost nor blench a jot.
> 'God who sets me to judge thee, meted out
> So much of judging faculty, no more:
> Ask him if I was slack in use thereof!'[1]

What makes Browning's examination of Christian
conceptions of the Supernatural completely convincing
in this mediation is both the fact that he expresses
these conceptions through a 17th-century pope and
that he expresses them with a restraint and sensitivity
quite alien to the tub-thumping rant of *Christmas-Eve.*
'So, it appears,' the Pope seems to say, 'but the intellect is limited, here we know in part only.' It is in fact,
his admission that we can never know God completely,
that makes his prayer to God so moving, and it is the

---

[1] *Ibid.*

exploratory thought of the passage – it is in no sense
dogmatic – that makes it alive.

O Thou, – as represented here to me
In such conception as my soul allows, –
Under Thy measureless, my atom width! –
Man's mind, what is it but a convex glass
Wherein are gathered all the scattered points
Picked out of the immensity of sky,
To re-unite there, be our heaven for earth,
Our known unknown, our God revealed to man?
Existent somewhere, somehow, as a whole;
Here, as a whole proportioned to our sense, –
There, (which is nowhere, speech must babble thus!)
In the absolute immensity, the whole
Appreciable solely by Thyself, –
Here, by the little mind of man, reduced
To littleness that suits his faculty . . .[1]

In Pompilia Browning has created another character
whose sanctity never detracts from her reality as a
human being. For the old Pope she is what gives life
its meaning.

It was not given Pompilia to know much,
Speak much, to write a book, to move mankind,
Be memorized by who records my time.
Yet if in purity and patience, if
In faith held fast despite the plucking fiend,
Safe like the signet stone with the new name
That saints are known by, – if in right returned
For wrong, most pardon for worst injury,
If there be any virtue, any praise, –
Then will this woman-child have proved – who knows? –
Just the one prize vouchsafed unworthy me,

[1] *Ibid.*

135

> Seven years a gardener of the untoward ground,
> I till, – this earth, my sweat and blood manure
> All the long day that barrenly grows dusk:
> At least one blossom makes me proud at eve
> Born 'mid the briers of my enclosure!
>
> . . . .
>
> My rose, I gather for the breast of God . . .[1]

Pompilia is also, in the perfection of her life, some
evidence for the existence of God and a significant
meaning latent in the confusion of our human predicament. Her perfection, Browning suggests, has been
brought about by the 'dread machinery' of suffering,
by the growing pains of life. In other poems, *Prospice*,
for instance, he expounds this same idea but with dogmatic stridency. Here it is stated with humility and is
acceptable.

> What lacks, then, of perfection fit for God
> But just the instance which this tale supplies
> Of love without a limit? So is strength,
> So is intelligence; let love be so,
> Unlimited in its self-sacrifice,
> Then is the tale true, and God shows complete.
> Beyond the tale, I reach into the dark,
> Feel what I cannot see, and still faith stands:
> I can believe this dread machinery
> Of sin and sorrow, would confound me else,
> Devised, – all pain, at most expenditure
> Of pain, by Who devised pain, – to evolve,
> By new machinery in counterpart,
> The moral qualities of man – how else?[2]

Like that of Pippa, the life of Pompilia fructifies in
the lives of others. Caponsacchi is changed by his love

[1] *Ibid.*   [2] *Ibid.*

for the martyred woman – it is the love denoted by the word Agapé – from a somewhat profligate dilettante into 'the soldier saint',

> When the first moan broke from the martyr-maid
> At that uncaging of the beasts, – made bare
> My athlete on the instant, gave such good
> Great undisguised leap over post and pale
> Right into the mid-cirque, free fighting-place.[1]

Pompilia ends her death-bed meditation, which is Book VII of the poem, with a thought of Caponsacchi and an extraordinarily convincing evocation of a relationship which has transcended temporal existence and the finite personality.

> In heaven we have the real and true and sure.
> 'Tis there they neither marry nor are given
> In marriage but are as the angels:
> . . . . . . how like Jesus Christ
> To say that! Marriage-making for the earth,
> With gold so much, – birth, power, repute so much,
> Or beauty, youth so much, in lack of these!
> Be as the angels rather, who, apart,
> Know themselves into one, are found at length
> Married, but marry never, no, nor give
> In marriage; they are man and wife at once
> When the true time is: here we have to wait
> Not so long neither! Could we by a wish
> Have what we will and get the future now,
> Would we wish ought done undone in the past?
> So, let him wait God's instant men call years;
> Meantime hold hard by truth and his great soul,
> Do out the duty! Through such souls alone
> God stooping shows sufficient of His light
> For us i' the dark to rise by. And I rise.[2]

[1] *Ibid.*   [2] *Pompilia* (Bk VII).

I have quoted fully from *The Ring and the Book* and hope that the passages I have quoted show that this work contains some of the poet's most profound and vital writing. The meditation of Pompilia and the Pope, together with Browning's *Invocation* to his dead wife are the most significant passages of the work. In these passages all his genius is involved. They exist on one level of inspiration and the reader has no need to cut his way through thickets of clever but dead language in order to reach five or ten lines of living poetry. In the other books one has to perform this kind of work. The reward, a passage which gives some unique illumination of depravity or beatitude, does not alter the fact that the effort of reaching it is uncongenial to the contemporary reader who both in the poem and the novel looks for brevity and compression. Nor, as in Wordsworth's *The Prelude*, are the flat passages of this poem an essential condition of its moments of inspiration, the runway as it were, from which the work becomes airborne. They are merely dead. In fact every reader of the poem must be his own anthologist. But whether one restricts one's reading to the Pope and Pompilia or reads attentively through the whole work and gathers what is alive from its infinite variety, the result must be rewarding.

II

In this section I am going to discuss three poems of Browning which although they are religious are not specifically concerned with any one religion. *An Epistle of Karshish, Cleon, Caliban upon Setebos* – in these poems we find Browning's most penetrating exploration of the supernatural world. He is concerned here with those areas of experience where such terms as 'personality', 'here and now', 'you and I' have a significance which is more strange and complex than their common usage.

The poems are dramatic monologues and Browning developed this form from the soliloquies of the Elizabethan and Jacobean drama, though it is used to perfection by Chaucer. The monologue enables Browning to present his characters with an unusual directness. They are not described at one remove. They reveal themselves under the stimulus of some exceptional circumstance or propitious moment. Their self-revelation is not the 'I am not what I seem' of the earlier Elizabethan dramatic convention, since they reveal to the reader duplicities and conflicting motives of which they are often quite unaware. For instance, the Duke of *My Last Duchess* communicates to the reader a shadow side of himself of which he is ignorant.

Browning peoples the solitude in which his personae have their being with presences which are no less real for being silent and invisible. He also creates for his personae a local habitation which is both a place in its own right at a particular moment of time and a reflection of personality. The Duke's art gallery, the moonlit, vinous street of *Fra Lippo Lippi*, the terrace and twilight of *Andrea del Sarto*, in these and many other poems, the scene emphasizes some essential flavour of the protagonist. And Browning's men and women – perhaps this is characteristic of any person of exceptional vitality – are both themselves and the manifestation of some particular tendency of their age.

Thus Karshish with his endurance, passionate curiosity and uneasy scepticism, is both himself and an expression of the perennial conflict between revealed and experimental truth; truth born from mystical experience and truth derived from scientific investigation.

The monologue is in the form of a letter which Karshish, who is on a pilgrimage of medical enquiry, writes to his master, Abib, from Bethany. Both the time of the poem, shortly before the sack of Jerusalem, and the hardship of the doctor's pilgrimage are given at the start of the poem, and given not only with great liveliness but with that economy which is characteristic of Browning's best work and enables him to communicate the substance of a novel in a few hundred lines.

> I have shed sweat enough, left flesh and bone
> On many a flinty furlong of this land.
> Also the country-side is all on fire
> With rumours of a marching hitherward –
> Some say Vespasian cometh, some, his son.
> A black lynx snarled and pricked a tufted ear;
> Lust of my blood inflamed his yellow balls:
> I cried and threw my staff and he was gone.

Karshish is a doctor and he keeps a constant watch on the external world in the interest of medical science –

> . . . there's a spider here
> Weaves no web, watches on the ledge of tombs,
> Sprinkled with mottles on an ash-grey back;
> Take five and drop them . . .

But into his world of empirical phenomena which can be understood in terms of cause and effect there intrudes 'one Lazarus, a Jew'. He purports to have been raised from the dead by 'a Nazarene physician of his

138

tribe', and he is an apparition quite inexplicable in terms of those scientific concepts by which Karshish both 'understands' and circumscribes the mystery of existence.

That is one theme of the poem, the impact of the supernatural upon a mind only aware – until this strange meeting – of natural phenomena. Browning shows with great skill – ' 'Tis but a case of mania – sub-induced by epilepsy' – the twists and turns by which Karshish tries to explain away a phenomenon which not only challenges the orderly picture he has made of reality, but the ability of the scientific intellect to determine what is real. Lazarus is an intrusion of the supernatural into the natural order of existence. He has had direct experience of that manifestation of the supernatural we call Christianity and states what he has experienced with a conviction which Karshish finds both fascinating and profoundly disturbing.

> The very God! think, Abib; dost thou think?
> So, the All-Great, were the All-Loving too –
> So, through the thunder comes a human voice
> Saying, 'O heart I made, a heart beats here!
> Face, my hands fashioned, see it in myself.
> Thou hast no power nor may'st conceive of mine,
> But love I gave thee, with Myself to love,
> And thou must love me who have died for thee!'
> The madman saith He said so: it is strange.

Lazarus is dismissed as 'the madman' but although the poem ends with uncertainty, Browning has made it clear that the physician's whole view of life has been disrupted; that like the Magi of Eliot's poem he can no longer be at ease in 'the old dispensations'.

But it is Lazarus himself and his experience that are

the most important theme of the poem and of particular interest today. Through Lazarus, Browning
examines the change of attitude and conventional
value which would occur if a finite human being while
still alive became conscious of the dimension of death,
and of being involved in a process which is neither
finite nor human.

> He holds on firmly to some thread of life –
> (It is the life to lead perforcedly)
> Which runs across some vast distracting orb
> Of glory on either side that meagre thread,
> Which, conscious of, he must not enter yet –
> The spiritual life around the earthly life!
> The law of that is known to him as this –
> His heart and brain move there, his feet stay here.

The life we enter at birth and leave at death and which
is conditioned by time and space is the 'thread'. This
thread is the linear existence which extends from
moment to moment in the everyday world. Normally
we are, as it were, fixated to this thread and consequently unaware that it is only a minute strip of
experience scissored out of the unlimited possibilities
of existence. Those unlimited possibilities are the 'vast
distracting orb of glory' which the thread runs across.
The orb can be thought of as death, eternity, or that
enlargement of experience referred to by William
Blake, 'If the doors of perception were cleansed, every
thing would appear to man as it is, infinite.'[1]

Mystics, seers, certain visionary poets, have direct
experience of this other dimension of being which is
traversed by the thread of linear existence. This ex-

[1] *The Marriage of Heaven and Hell.*

perience modifies their behaviour, and is the perennial theme of their teaching and writing. In Lazarus, Browning portrays a man who has known the 'vast distracting orb' with exceptional intensity and because of an exceptional experience.

> The law of that is known to him as this –
> His heart and brain move there, his feet stay here.

Except in isolated moments of dream, vision, clairvoyance, human beings are for the most part subject to the horizontal line of temporal existence. They are only open to those stimuli which are given to their senses at the present moment, though they can remember past experience, that is to say some part of the thread already travelled, and anticipate the future, some small portion of the thread's further extension. But Lazarus has immediate knowledge of the 'orb' which the thread crosses. Consequently 'impulses' strike at him vertically from those dimensions which are above and below his life in time and space.

> So is the man perplext with impulses
> Sudden to start off crosswise, not straight on,
> Proclaiming what is Right and Wrong across –
> And not along – this black thread through the blaze –
> 'It should be' balked by 'here it cannot be.'

He has died and returned to life and this experience has made him acutely aware of the hiatus that exists between time and eternity. Since he is not conditioned by the logic of the horizontal thread but knows those vertical impulses which intersect time from eternity he has standards of right and wrong which, like those expressed by Christ in the Gospels, are quite alien to current morality. Indeed his sense of value is so radically different from that of the everyday world that Karshish almost believes he is an idiot.

> The man is witless of the size, the sum,
> The value in proportion of all things,
> Or whether it be little or be much.
> Discourse to him of prodigious armaments
> Assembled to besiege his city now,
> And of the passing of a mule with gourds –
> 'Tis one!

But it is not idiocy which makes Lazarus indifferent to the imminent fall of Jerusalem, but his knowledge that we are involved both in time and eternity, and that events which have great temporal importance may be quite insignificant in the dimensions beyond time. On the other hand, acts which appear trivial here and now – to our surface apprehension – may have an eternal resonance.

> Should his child sicken unto death, – why, look
> For scarce abatement of his cheerfulness,
> Or pretermission of his daily craft –
> While a word, gesture, glance, from that same child
> At play or in the school or laid asleep,
> Will start him to an agony of fear . . .

Lazarus's awareness of eternity gives him an immense concern and reverence for all living creatures,

> he loves both old and young,
> Able and weak – affects the very brutes
> And birds – how say I? flowers of the field –.

Like Blake, who had the same double vision he realizes the infinite significance of finite creation, that

A horse misused upon the Road
Calls to Heaven for Human blood . . .[1]

However, Lazarus has known the timeless dimension through the intervention of Christ, not through some innate aptitude, or slow spiritual development which he has himself initiated. T. S. Eliot writes of the strenuous cultivation of mystical insight in the fifth section of *The Dry Salvages*.[2] It is 'an occupation for the saint'.

> But to apprehend
> The point of intersection of the timeless
> With time, is an occupation for the saint —
> No occupation either, but something given
> And taken, in a lifetime's death in love,
> Ardour and selflessness and self-surrender.

Lazarus has reached this state of beatific vision by a short cut and without having travelled the difficult road which leads to it. In a sense he is where he has not yet arrived, knows a state of intensity and wholeness for which he has not undergone the appropriate maturation. Consequently he longs,

> For that same death which will restore his being
> To equilibrium, body loosening soul
> Divorced even now by premature full growth . . .

He longs for death since his awareness of eternity is premature and unbearable.

As I said before, in the range and quality of his psychological and metaphysical exploration Browning is our contemporary. Through Lazarus he expresses the

---

[1] *Auguries of Innocence.*
[2] *Four Quartets* (Faber, 1944).

rift which may lie between a man's or woman's intuitive or imaginative awareness both of eternity and psychic wholeness and their actual personality, finite and imperfect. This conflict has only recently become articulate, at least in the quasi-scientific language of psychology.

'Human kind', writes T. S. Eliot, 'cannot bear very much reality.'[1] Lazarus has known too much reality. Since his personality is inadequate to his knowledge, it is a question of enduring the almost intolerable tension of finite and infinite existence, and of 'prone submission' to the heavenly will.

In a later poem, *Bishop Blougram's Apology*,[2] Browning makes a further statement of his belief in the limitations of human consciousness, and the fact that since we are not strong enough to bear any fullness of knowledge of 'what is' we shelter ourselves from its impact by convenient fictions. For the most part the poem is an interesting but rather lengthy self-revelation by a wise and extremely subtle Catholic bishop to a sceptical journalist. But in one critical passage the poet becomes totally involved in the poem.

> Pure faith indeed – you know not what you ask!
> Naked belief in God the Omnipotent,
> Omniscient, Omnipresent, sears too much
> The sense of conscious creatures to be borne.

'Faith' is a word which can be interpreted in many ways. It can suggest an intuitive or imaginative act by which we are able to bridge the gap between life and death, time and eternity, the finite 'one' and infinite

[1] *Burnt Norton* (*Four Quartets*, Faber, 1944).
[2] *Men and Women.*

144

'all'; and bridge this gap without any sensory evidence. In Browning's passage it is equated with belief and suggests a knowledge of God, not known at one remove through concept or symbol, but arising out of immediate experience. Such an experience can be intolerable since it means a yoking of the finite and inadequate human ego to an energy which is both impersonal and infinite. It can, in fact, result in a complete fragmentation of personality – as if a small cup attempted to contain the entire sea. Perhaps this is why Christ, who had an exceptionally full communion with this omnipotence, is always careful not to identify himself with God – as a human creature. 'Not I,' he reiterates through the Gospels, 'but the Father who sent me . . . not I but the Father, he doeth these things.'

In poem after poem Browning insists that this duality of finite and infinite, one and all, is a condition of our human predicament. Psychological growth depends on our becoming conscious of this predicament and making creative use of the tension such knowledge must entail. But 'human kind cannot bear very much reality', so both external nature and the earthiness or animality which is part of our human nature shield us from intimacy with the Divine.

> Some think, Creation's meant to show him forth:
> I say, it's meant to hide him all it can,
> And that's what all the blessed Evil's for.
> Its use in time is to environ us,
> Our breath, our drop of dew, with shield enough
> Against that sight till we can bear its stress.
> Under a vertical sun, the exposed brain
> And lidless eye and disemprisoned heart

145

Less certainly would wither up at once
Than mind, confronted with the truth of Him.[1]

Creation, the phenomena of nature and the natural man are not thought of here as a showing forth of God in the Wordsworthian sense. They are a screen which shields us from the divine vision which would be too overwhelming for our undeveloped consciousness; shields us until we have grown strong enough to endure some partial awareness of supernatural reality. Such a growth of awareness and the strength to bear its inevitable tensions are for Browning an essential meaning of existence. It is the building while yet alive of D. H. Lawrence's 'Ship of Death', some essence of the human being which can weather eternity. Just as in the womb the foetus develops organs necessary for the temporal world, here in time we must evolve a spiritual body appropriate to eternity.

Creation is intended, so Blougram says, not so much to manifest as to hide its Creator, 'And that's what all the blessed Evil's for'. This is one of Browning's most cryptic statements and offers many potential meanings. Here is one possibility. Creation should shield us against whatever reality is signified by the word 'God' until we are strong enough to discard its protection and endure more directly some part of the divine vision. But Creation can be used not as a temporary shield but a permanent refuge, in other words as a means of permanently avoiding that growth of consciousness which Browning believes is the point of being human. In an earlier poem, *The Bishop Orders His Tomb at St Praxed's Church*, Browning describes

[1] *Bishop Blougram's Apology.*

146

a man who has abused nature in just this way. As he lies dying in his favourite church, surrounded by his illegitimate sons, the Bishop holds fast to those finite compulsions of his lifetime, which have proved an impenetrable shield against the life of the spirit. It's a question of an expensive tomb in a desirable position; for at the very edge of death, he can think of no purpose or satisfaction other than those he promises his sons if they will 'do the right thing by his carcass',

> Horses for ye, and brown Greek manuscripts,
> And mistresses with great smooth marbly limbs?

I mentioned that for Wordsworth Nature showed forth the Infinite, was the manifestation of a power which used but exceeded her phenomena. But in the *Immortality Ode* Wordsworth attributes to a secondary and more lowly aspect of nature which he calls Earth, a task very similar to Browning's Creation which is meant to hide man from the unbearable intensity of the Divine,

> Earth fills her lap with pleasures of her own;
> Yearnings she hath in her own natural kind,
> And even with something of a mother's mind,
>   And no unworthy aim,
>   The homely Nurse doth all she can
> To make her foster-child, her inmate Man,
>   Forget the glories he hath known,
> And that imperial palace whence he came.

Browning writes of 'God', Wordsworth of 'glories' and the 'imperial palace', but both poets agree that we are protected by both human and external nature from too great an intimacy with supernatural power.

They agree because they are both visionary poets

and as such affirm – without empirical evidence – certain perennial realities of the human situation. It is only recently and in our own age that these truths have been stated with a basis of empirical evidence and in language nearer to the prose of science than the images and aphorisms of poetry and religion. Two books by Aldous Huxley, for example, *The Doors of Perception* and *Heaven and Hell*, examine from the standpoint of contemporary psychology and experiment some of the problems of *Karshish* and the *Immortality Ode*. Incidentally, it is probable that such works of psychological and metaphysical exploration provide in our day a more profound elucidation of visionary poetry than any other type of writing. Certainly *The Doors of Perception*[1] is extremely relevant both to *Karshish* and the *Immortality Ode*. In the light of his dangerous experiments with the drug Mescalin, Huxley suggests that our brain acts as a kind of shield or rather protective filter to ward off certain intensities of experience which might either 'sear too much the sense of conscious creatures to be borne', or be so intrinsically satisfying as to make unimportant any adjustment to the everyday world and response to its claims by directed activity. When the action of this filter – it is apparently localized in the frontal lobes of the brain – is inhibited by Mescalin then such everyday phenomena as a bowl of flowers or a trouser crease can so blaze with significance that action becomes without meaning and only contemplation an appropriate response. Huxley divines, and with something approaching scientific method, just that duality of experience, that capacity to apprehend both a finite and

[1] Chatto (1954).

148

infinite significance which is a theme of Wordsworth, Browning and William Blake. And he suggests a psychosomatic basis to that element in human nature which both Wordsworth and Browning believed protected our immature consciousness from an unbearable intensity of vision. Poets, as I have said elsewhere, are among the most significant explorers of the inner life.

Both in the range and nature of its thought *Cleon*[1] is a companion piece to *Karshish*. But whereas *Karshish* examines the change in attitude and behaviour which would result from a realization while yet alive of the dimension of death, in *Cleon* Browning speculates on the state of mind of a highly sensitive and intelligent man who has no inkling of an order of existence other than the material world. Once more the poem is in the form of a letter, this time from a famous artist, philosopher and poet to a royal patron who has sent him gifts and asked him certain questions. Many of Browning's characters have a double significance. Cleon's predicament is both that of an individual of any age, and of the Graeco-Roman culture which at the time of St Paul had lost its spiritual impulse and in a kind of doldrums awaited that showing forth of the divine we associate with Christianity. In such a time, as Yeats suggests in *The Second Coming*,[2] 'The best lack all conviction'. The aged Cleon considers the variety of temporal achievement. But neither material power, art, nor philosophical speculation are able to satisfy human aspiration.

[1] *Men and Women.*
[2] *Michael Robartes and the Dancer* (1921) (*The Collected Poems of W. B. Yeats*).

> I can write love-odes – thy fair slave's an ode.
> I get to sing of love, when grown too grey
> For being beloved: she turns to that young man
> The muscles all a-ripple on his back.

Yeats understood this situation and, unlike Cleon, the way out of it.

> An aged man is but a paltry thing,
> A tattered coat upon a stick, unless
> Soul clap its hands and sing, and louder sing
> For every tatter in its mortal dress . . .[1]

It is possible to rejoice in 'the rags and tatters' because one can see through their rents. Old age can bring not only bodily decrepitude but spiritual insight and knowledge of an order of existence to which physical decrepitude is irrelevant. Cleon has no such realization. He is time-fixated, consequently all human activity is end-stopped by death and basically futile.

> 'But,' sayest thou – (and I marvel, I repeat,
> To find thee tripping on a mere word) 'what
> Thou writest, paintest, stays: that does not die:
> Sappho survives, because we sing her songs,
> And Æschylus, because we read his plays!'
> Why, if they live still, let them come and take
> Thy slave in my despite – drink from thy cup –
> Speak in my place.

He divines that consciousness is the unique faculty of men and women:

> – had Zeus then questioned thee
> 'Wilt thou go on a step, improve on this,
> Do more for visible creatures than is done?'

[1] *Sailing to Byzantium, op. cit.*

> Thou wouldst have answered, 'Ay, by making each
> Grow conscious in himself – by that alone . . .'

He also realizes that the point of human existence may well be the enlargement of this consciousness:

> . . . let him critically learn
> How he lives; and, the more he gets to know
> Of his own life's adaptabilities,
> The more joy-giving will his life become.
> The man who hath this quality, is best.

Consciousness makes us aware

> That there's a world of capability
> For joy, spread round about us, meant for us . . .

But since both joy and consciousness are bounded by that death which Cleon believes is a final full stop, they are futile. Moreover an increase in consciousness makes us aware of a range of experience and knowledge which is not only beyond our present and finite scope, but beyond our potential scope. Cleon does not believe that growth towards death is also growth towards some extra-temporal dimension where our knowledge and experience will find their meaning. Development, symbolized by the King's tower, is without meaning

> alas!
> The soul now climbs it just to perish there . . . .

Since it only makes us more acutely aware of the frustration of human existence and that development is without goal, Cleon is led to deny the value of spiritual evolution.

> And so a man can use but a man's joy
> While he sees God's. Is it, for Zeus to boast

'See, man, how happy I live, and despair – '
. . . .
Most progress is most failure! thou sayest well.

The growth of consciousness makes one more fully aware of the possibilities of existence. But it is paralleled, this growth, by old age, and old age makes it progressively less possible to enjoy any finite experience, let alone that fuller scope of experience revealed by a developing consciousness. Browning in this poem gives a most poignant analysis of the predicament of the time-fixated man. If consciousness evolves but remains unconscious of that extra-temporal dimension, which Blake called Jerusalem and Yeats Byzantium, then its evolution can only multiply merely temporal needs. But the increasing age which accompanies this growth of time-fixated consciousness makes the realization of such needs physically impossible. Man is condemned to a process of gradual self-suffocation:

> . . . my fate is deadlier still, –
> In this, that every day my sense of joy
> Grows more acute, my soul (intensified
> In power and insight) more enlarged, more keen;
> While every day my hairs fall more and more,
> My hand shakes, and the heavy years increase –
> The horror quickening still from year to year,
> The consummation coming past escape
> When I shall know most, and yet least enjoy –.

Blake writes in *The Marriage of Heaven and Hell*,

For the cherub with his flaming sword is hereby commanded to leave his guard at the tree of life; and when he does, the whole creation will be consumed and appear infinite and holy, whereas it now appears finite & corrupt.

This will come to pass by an improvement of sensual enjoyment.

Blake realized that through an enlargement of consciousness 'corruption could put on incorruption', and the infinite significance of the finite creature become apparent. Because he cannot achieve this double vision, Cleon, for all his intelligence and sensitivity, is, like Proust's Baron de Charlus, 'crucified on the rock of pure matter'. One thinks of a foetus developing in the womb without a material world to be born into and whose eyes and limbs would in consequence bear relevance to nothing. Cleon is aware of the growth of spiritual qualities. But since he is unaware of a spiritual existence, whether in or outside time, to which they might be appropriate, these qualities are meaningless. The meaning is hinted at towards the end of the poem but dismissed by Cleon — he is a rational man and there is just not sufficient evidence.

> It is so horrible,
> I dare at times imagine to my need
> Some future state revealed to us by Zeus,
> Unlimited in capability
> For joy, as this is in desire for joy,
> To seek which, the joy-hunger forces us.
> That, stung by straitness of our life, made strait
> On purpose to make sweet the life at large —
> Freed by the throbbing impulse we call death
> We burst there as the worm into the fly,
> Who, while a worm still, wants his wings. But, no!
> Zeus has not yet revealed it; and, alas!
> He must have done so — were it possible!

The 'future state revealed to us by Zeus' is known and directly by Lazarus. But Cleon is too steeped in the culture of his age, too identified with its conventions of thought and feeling for any new revelation to find living room in his over-furnished mind. The new revelation – as in the *Epistle of Karshish* – is Christian. The King has mentioned his meeting with St Paul in his letter and asks Cleon to make a further contact with the apostle. There is both irony and pathos in Cleon's scornful rejection of the man who could perhaps have made a living confirmation of that other order of existence for which the artist has such deep need.

> Thou canst not think a mere barbarian Jew,
> As Paulus proves to be, one circumcised,
> Hath access to a secret shut from us?
> Thou wrongest our philosophy, O king,
> In stooping to inquire of such an one,
> As if his answer could impose at all.
> He writeth, doth he? well, and he may write.
> Oh, the Jew findeth scholars! certain slaves
> Who touched on this same isle, preached him and Christ;
> And (as I gathered from a bystander)
> Their doctrines could be held by no sane man.

Deprived of 'the throbbing impulse we call death', I mean some outgoing purpose which is not end-stopped by mortality, then human desire must either regress – one thinks of the dying bishop – or, as with Cleon, lose all intensity. In his old age Cleon exists in a sad no-man's land between the end of time and an eternity in which he does not believe. His emotions relate neither to Eros – he has outgrown physical desire – nor to Agapé, since that developed love seeks neither to possess nor be possessed and is therefore relevant to the eternity in which the sage has no belief. He looks at his present that 'white she-slave', 'one lyric woman, in her crocus vest' neither with desire nor compassion but the eye of a bored connoisseur.

In *Cleon* and *Karshish* Browning expresses his belief that we are not circumscribed by our finite human ego or our physical presence in time but are involved in a dimension which exceeds time, space and personality. Through the Lazarus of *Karshish* and a passage of *Bishop Blougram's Apology* he shows the difficulty and tension which must be involved if we experience this duality of human existence – with any fullness. In *Cleon* he shows the frustration which ensues if we bypass this duality and repress any awareness of the supernatural.

But what do we really know of God? To what extent must any conception of the supernatural and the infinite be a projection of some 'natural' desire or some thought which is merely finite? That is one of the themes of a remarkable poem, *Caliban upon Setebos*,[1] whose epigraph 'Thou thoughtest that I was altogether such an one as thyself' suggests that man must project some quality of himself on to the supernatural.

In Caliban, Browning has anticipated the discovery of modern anthropologists and psychologists; that the 'ego', the sense of 'me-ness', depends on a certain degree of maturation. A young child will not say 'I ate too many sweets' or 'I was naughty' but 'Johnny ate too many sweets' or 'Johnny was naughty'. A primitive aboriginal will often say 'The killing of a buck took place near (or through) this man' rather than 'I killed a buck'. In the same way Caliban talks about himself for the most part in the third person.

[1] *Dramatis Personae.*

'Will sprawl, now that the heat of the day is best,
Flat on his belly in the pit's much mire . . .

The poem is a study of a creature who exists somewhere between man and beast. Through Caliban,
rooted as he is in the natural universe, Browning
celebrates the infinite variety of creation.

Yon auk, one fire-eye in a ball of foam,
That floats and feeds; a certain badger brown
He hath watched hunt with that slant white-wedge eye
By moonlight . . .

The most interesting theme of the poem is the
evolution of religious consciousness. Caliban is brood-
ing about Setebos, the god-demon of his mother the
witch who receives this cryptic comment from Pros-
pero, 'The blue-eyed hag was hither brought with
child, and here was left by the sailors.' Setebos is both
Caliban's obsession and torment.

Setebos, Setebos, and Setebos!
'Thinketh He dwelleth i' the cold o' the moon.

Browning has no illusions about the 'freedom' of primitive man and Caliban's life is hag-ridden by guilts and
anxiety. 'Thou thoughtest that I was altogether such
an one as thyself': Setebos is Caliban's tormentor since
the half-man has projected on to this god-demon all his
own dissatisfaction and ferocity. The god-demon is
restless and incomplete. He has created the world as a
kind of salve; it is a plaything with which he both
satisfies his cruelty and wards off anxiety and boredom.

Put case, unable to be what I wish,
I yet could make a live bird out of clay:
Would not I take clay, pinch my Caliban

Able to fly? – for, there, see, he hath wings,
And great comb like the hoopoe's to admire,
And there, a sting to do his foes offence,
There, and I will that he begin to live,
Fly to yon rock-top, nip me off the horns
Of grigs high up that make the merry din,
Saucy through their veined wings, and mind me not.
In which feat, if his leg snapped, brittle clay,
And he lay stupid-like, – why, I should laugh;
And if he, spying me, should fall to weep,
Beseech me to be good, repair his wrong,
Bid his poor leg smart less or grow again, –
Well, as the chance were, this might take or else
Not take my fancy: I might hear his cry,
And give the manikin three legs for his one,
Or pluck the other off, leave him like an egg,
And lessoned he was mine and merely clay.

In its conception of a God who is amoral, capriciously
cruel and in need of man's constant self-abasement,
that passage is close both to some early conception of
the Jewish Jehovah and the nihilism of Gloster's

> As flies to wanton boys, are we to the Gods, –
> They kill us for their sport.[1]

The poem is a study of the evolution of religious consciousness. Just as Browning had outgrown the Dissent
of his mother (*vide Christmas-Eve*) so Caliban has partially outgrown the monomania and bigotry of Setebos, otherwise he would not have such a clear idea of
the god's limitations. Partially outgrown; he still projects his own bestiality and cruelty on to his god.
Caliban has wished off his own darkness on to Setebos.

---

[1] William Shakespeare, *King Lear*, IV, i.

Consequently the half-man is superior to his god and Setebos is jealous of the superiority of his own creation.

> Oh, He hath made things worthier than Himself,
> And envieth that, so helped, such things do more
> Than He who made them! What consoles but this?
> That they, unless through Him, do nought at all,
> And must submit: what other use in things?
> 'Hath cut a pipe of pithless elder-joint
> That, blown through, gives exact the scream o' the jay
> When from her wing you twitch the feathers blue:
> Sound this, and little birds that hate the jay
> Flock within stone's throw, glad their foe is hurt:
> Put case such pipe could prattle and boast forsooth
> 'I catch the birds, I am the crafty thing,
> I make the cry my maker cannot make
> With his great round mouth; he must blow through
>   mine!'
> Would not I smash it with my foot? So He.

Caliban expresses not only the evolution of animal into man, but of human consciousness. His potential but not fully achieved 'self' is able to see the inadequacy of Setebos and conceive a higher conception of God. The primitive undeveloped side of his nature still grovels before the demon-god it has created. Perhaps what keeps Setebos alive is Caliban's own cruelty, suggested by such lines as

> . . . the scream o' the jay
> When from her wing you twitch the feathers blue . . .

Certainly his fear of Setebos whom he feels bears him a personal grudge is as real as his understanding of the god's limitations; this understanding being a major reason for the grudge.

'Saith He is terrible: watch His feats in proof!
One hurricane will spoil six good months' hope.
He hath a spite against me, that I know . . .

The new conception of God which Caliban is
evolving he calls 'The Quiet':

There may be something quiet o'er His head,
Out of His reach, that feels nor joy nor grief,
Since both derive from weakness in some way.
I joy because the quails come; would not joy
Could I bring quails here when I have a mind:
This Quiet, all it hath a mind to, doth.
'Esteemeth stars the outposts of its couch,
But never spends much thought nor care that way.

Since 'The Quiet' is not a projection on to the supernatural of purely human emotions but is a reality
beyond the fallible Caliban and the god he has made
in his own image, it 'feels nor joy nor grief, Since both
derive from weakness in some way'.

The poem's most startling passage – it is perhaps too
far ranging in its thought and suggestiveness to be
associated with Caliban – is the image of the fish. It
lives in a spike, or small current of icy cold water, surrounded on either side by pleasant 'lukewarm brine'.
It longs for and perpetually attempts to enter this more
hospitable climate. But because of some intrinsic
quality of its nature – lungs, gills – it is unable to do so
and must always retreat to the cold stream it dislikes.
Browning uses this creature and its environment as an
image for the creation of the world by Setebos. The
God has made the world as a compensation for his
inability to live in the environment he desires. But the
image is more significant in its reference to man's

divided consciousness. We long to escape from the cold spike of water, that is to say the limitations of our fallen selves and environment, but have not undergone the death in life, the psychic development which would enable us to be at home in another mode of existence.

> 'Thinketh, it came of being ill at ease:
> He hated that He cannot change His cold,
> Nor cure its ache. 'Hath spied an icy fish
> That longed to 'scape the rock-stream where she lived,
> And thaw herself within the lukewarm brine
> O' the lazy sea her stream thrusts far amid,
> A crystal spike 'twixt two warm walls of wave;
> Only she ever sickened, found repulse
> At the other kind of water, not her life,
> (Green-dense and dim-delicious, bred o' the sun)
> Flounced back from bliss she was not born to breathe,
> And in her old bounds buried her despair,
> Hating and loving warmth alike: so He.

Because of the extremity of the division within himself Caliban is acutely conscious of the need to evolve. Like the fish he longs to enter that freer and more lucid mode of being symbolized by the 'lukewarm brine'. He also longs for a development in his awareness of God; for the persecutory Setebos to change into 'The Quiet'.

> 'Conceiveth all things will continue thus,
> And we shall have to live in fear of Him
> So long as He lives, keeps His strength: no change,
> If He have done His best, make no new world
> To please Him more, so leave off watching this, --
> If He surprise not even the Quiet's self
> Some strange day, – or, suppose, grow into it

As grubs grow butterflies: else, here are we,
And there is He, and nowhere help at all.

This poem and the other great religious poems of
Browning form a body of work which in its examination of man's relationship to God and to his neighbour
is as searching and far ranging as that of any poet in
our language. The tentative but exceedingly interesting conclusions that Browning reaches are in harmony
with the psychological climate of our own age. He
reaches them by a resolute questioning of certain preconceptions and ingrained habits of thought; a questioning which many of us may find of value.

NOTE
Many poets and, in our own age, psychologists continue an ancient tradition of wisdom once repressed by
orthodox Christianity. Certainly there is a correspondence between *Caliban upon Setebos* and the belief of
many Gnostic sects that this world was not created by
the Highest God, 'The Unknown Father', but by the
demiourgos, Iadalbaoth, who was proud, savage and
ignorant. He disliked and wished to destroy his creation.
However the Highest God through his female quality,
Sophia, sent the serpent to persuade man to eat of the
Tree of Knowledge, forbidden by Iadalbaoth who
wished to keep mankind ignorant and impotent. Wisdom enabled man to defy Iadalbaoth; the Old Testament records this struggle. Finally the Higher God
sent Christ to save man from the demiourgos.[1]

[1] Kurt Seligman, *The History of Magic* (New York, Pantheon
Books, 1948).

Chapter Five

Technique and Imagery

> But Art, – wherein man nowise speaks to men,
> Only to mankind, – Art may tell a truth
> Obliquely, do the thing shall breed the thought,
> Nor wrong the thought, missing the mediate word.
> > *The Ring and the Book*, Bk XII.

It is impossible to separate a poem from its technique
or a poet's technique from his feeling and thought –
indeed from his total achievement. It is impossible
(although the attempt is often made) to write about
technique in isolation from this totality unless one is
willing to reduce a poem to a dead exercise.

I once edited an anthology to which contributions
were invited in the public press. Out of the four or five
thousand contributions we printed about sixty, of the
sixty some fifty-five were by poets of reputation. The
choice did not, I believe, depend on a conservative bias
but the rarity of poetic talent. Such talent is not
synonymous with deep feeling and thought. Some of
the rejected pieces were extremely thoughtful. Many
contributors underlined the deep feeling they tried to
express by a covering letter – I wrote this when my

child died or my wife went off with the milkman. But despite the power of the feeling and thought, the result was not a poem. The pieces lacked technique and technique is the mysterious X in the artistic equation. Just as electricity is changed into light by an extremely accurate arrangement of glass and wire filament, so feeling and thought can be changed into poetry by an extremely accurate arrangement of words which both focuses and transforms their energies. A poem needs deep thought and feeling. It needs that descent into the unconscious whereby one may confront the source of imaginative power – a descent which often depends upon difficult childhood experience. But although such a descent may be a condition of a certain quality of wisdom it will not bring about poetry unless it happens to a person who possesses poetic technique. No doubt many of us have felt the nostalgia of this anonymous quatrain,

> O western wind, when wilt thou blow
> That the small rain down can rain?
> Christ, if my love were in my arms,
> And I in my bed again.

But few people can recreate their nostalgia by such an exact arrangement of words and so doing change it from the personal utterance of a letter to the universal statement of a poem. One realizes the dependence of the poem on word precision if one changes some of the phrases of that quatrain – 'western wind' to 'wind of the west', for instance, 'bed' to 'double bed'. The poem is organic and bleeds to death under drastic surgery.

We may understand the personal disturbance which

may lead to poetic creation, the effect on Byron, Browning, Rimbaud, Lawrence, of the mother; the relationship of Hallam's death to *In Memoriam*. But poetic technique remains as inexplicable as its ability to make something of extreme significance out of apparent ordinariness. I say 'apparent' ordinariness because although what can be given of a memorable passage of poetry by a prose paraphrase may seem humdrum enough, this means that the prose has encompassed a mere fraction of the poem as the poem fans out into innumerable possibilities. One gets little idea of Macbeth's famous soliloquy 'Tomorrow and tomorrow and tomorrow' by a prose resumé that the king is utterly disillusioned, finds no meaning in life and wishes to die. Great poetry catches into the patterned (I mean rhythmic and rhymed) fabric of its language both thought and feeling and so doing creates a third thing, the poem, which cannot be explained solely in terms of thought and feeling.

Although one cannot say just why certain people are gifted with poetic technique, if they do possess it then it enables them to infuse some essence of themselves into their writing. Paradoxically it is this very individual stamp of the work of a great poet which makes his work, if not impersonal, of general significance, and distinguishes it from the anonymity of minor writers. A poem is a dialogue; since a dialogue can only take place between two people, the poet, however subtly dispersed among his personae, must be present within his work.

Such presence need not depend upon the direct personal utterance that we find in some of Shakespeare's sonnets or a poem like Yeats's *The Spur* —

You think it horrible that lust and rage
Should dance attention upon my old age;
They were not such a plague when I was young;
What else have I to spur me into song?[1]

There has been a tendency to equate poetry with the personal lyric and relegate Browning to a minor role because, so we are told, he wrote very few poems in this form. I think this is a quite arbitrary misconception of poetry and also a misunderstanding of Browning's work. It is true that unlike Yeats he rarely writes a poem which is a direct expression of his own passionate feeling unalloyed with speculation. I myself can only think of one such work of his which seems completely successful. The sonnet occasioned by Edward FitzGerald's cantankerous stricture on the poet's dead wife[2] has that blend of rage and grandeur we find in many of Yeats's poems:

Kicking you seems the common lot of curs –
While more appropriate greeting lends you grace:
Surely to spit there glorifies your face –
Spitting – from lips once sanctified by Hers.

But to say that he rarely makes such a direct emotional utterance only means that though a deeply thoughtful and strongly emotional poet, for Browning thought and emotion work together. Indeed it is the counterpoint between strong thought and feeling which gives to such personal works as *Two in the Campagna*, or the *Invocation* to Elizabeth Barrett their unique quality. I have already discussed these poems in the chapter which deals with Browning's love poetry. *Two in the Campagna* is both an affirmation of his love for his

[1] *Last Poems* (1936–1939). [2] See above, p. 55.

wife and a meditation upon the nature of love, indeed human relationship itself. His deep feeling for his wife is counterpointed with a realization that grows as the poem proceeds of the paradox of relationship. It is our communion with each other that gives life its meaning and seems to be a meaning of life, but this communion is never complete.

A quality of Browning's poetry and one which has had a profound if unacknowledged influence on the work of this decade is its conversational intimacy. Whether he is talking directly as himself or, as in *My Last Duchess* and *Andrea del Sarto*, through some persona he makes us feel that in a finite moment of infinite significance, we are listening to a living person and catching – such is his technical skill – not only a tone of voice, but the changing movement of hand and face and some indefinable human essence which can neither be heard nor seen.

> I wonder do you feel to-day
>> As I have felt, since, hand in hand,
> We sat down on the grass, to stray
>> In spirit better through the land,
> This morn of Rome and May?

Although addressed to his wife, the quiet conversational tone of 'I wonder do you feel to-day' involves the reader. Important revolutions do not depend upon verbal pyrotechnics but upon subtle changes of tone and rhythm. Some of Browning's poems create a greater intimacy between himself and the reader than the work of any poet with the exception of William Blake and Donne. This intimacy does not depend upon the loose confessional free verse of which Walt Whitman is the master and such writers as Alan Ginsberg and Gregory Corso the dead but hysterical end. A poem like *Two in the Campagna* is formal both in rhyme and metre. The sense of conversational intimacy, of our catching the development of the poet's thought as he thinks aloud, is created by an extremely skilful use of 'pause' and 'run on' – I hesitate to use 'caesura' and 'enjambment' since Browning, although a supreme technician, appears to have had little use for such terms. In *Two in the Campagna* the poet likens the subtle twists and turns of his thought to a spider's winding and delicate thread.

> Help me to hold it: first it left
>> The yellowing fennel, run to seed
> There, branching from the brickwork's cleft,
>> Some old tomb's ruin: yonder weed
> Took up the floating weft,
>
> Where one small orange cup amassed
>> Five beetles, – blind and green they grope
> Among the honey-meal, – and last
>> Everywhere on the grassy slope
> I traced it. Hold it fast!

'Help me to hold it'. That such words have poetic significance depends upon their position in the metrical and emotional scheme of *Two in the Campagna*. Browning will often place a sparse colloquial statement at the end or beginning of some verse of great rhythmical subtlety so that, like Lear's 'Pray you undo this button', a line of ordinary speech is invested with exceptional pathos and meaning. On the other hand his metrical pattern is brought to the heel of everyday humanity by common speech. By variations of movement and pause, by the contrast of colloquial and 'heightened' language, by his formal but infinitely varied metres Browning seems to communicate the living movement of thought and speech.

The later poetry of Yeats is also close to the movement of thought and the accents of daily speech – but with a difference.

> I must lie down where all the ladders start,
> In the foul rag-and-bone shop of the heart.

Those last lines of *The Circus Animals' Desertion*[1] are an exact expression of Yeats's mood. They state a perennial problem – our need to slough off every rhetorical disguise and come to terms with our extremely fallible humanity. But Yeats accepts his fallibility with such stoical grandeur that the act of acceptance becomes an act of dismissal. Perhaps fully to acknowledge is to win free of the less pleasing aspects of ourselves. But it is difficult to talk about Yeats's finest poems without such words as 'grandeur' and 'magnificence' hovering behind our speech. There are many assertions of human and personal conflict in the work of this great poet but they are made with such passionate if tragic irony that they suggest transcendence. This transcendence is both of human fallibility and death itself.

> *Cast a cold eye*
> *On life, on death.*
> *Horseman, pass by!*[2]

It is an impertinence to try and assess the comparative value of poets who have achieved a certain stature.

[1] *Last Poems, op. cit.*   [2] *Under Ben Bulben* (1938), *ibid.*

Yeats regards his everyday humanity from a detached,
at times ironic standpoint, so that Yeats, the man, becomes almost a character in the spectacle recorded by
Yeats, the poet. Browning also has detachment and
irony in his best poems. But whether he is writing
about himself or other people, his attitude in his most
significant work is that of a fallible human being whose
judgement is no less acute for being uncertain. It is not
meant to be a disparagement of Yeats if I say that
Browning seldom uses and never with success the
dramatic personal gesture, or the 'heroic mask'.

> A barnacle goose
> Far up in the stretches of night; night splits and the
>   dawn breaks loose;
> I, through the terrible novelty of light, stalk on, stalk
>   on;
> Those great sea-horses bare their teeth and laugh at the
>   dawn.[1]

Yeats introduces himself into the landscape at the end
of *High Talk*, but by some subtle nuance of language
(it is partly the force of the verb 'stalk') dehumanizes
himself, so that we do not think of Mr Yeats taking a
picturesque morning walk but of man himself as part
of the immense light-washed process of nature. Perhaps in the last resort our humanity is only an incident
in the soul's progress between birth and death, and
Yeats's greatest achievement is to affirm the soul and
to make us aware of that element of men and women
which is not limited by mortality. Although Browning
is also aware of this spiritual significance his particular
theme is our complex and troubled humanity. The last

[1] *High Talk, ibid.*

two verses of *Two in the Campagna*, for instance, communicate the tentative movement of thought, the sense we have of pushing our thought to some final conclusion, of following relationship to some absolute consummation, only to find that once more the goal has eluded us, and we are left in the uncertain half-way house of our everyday selves.

> Just when I seemed about to learn!
> Where is the thread now? Off again!
> The old trick! Only I discern –
> Infinite passion and the pain
> Of finite hearts that yearn.

I have already commented on this passage. It does not – as with some of the finest passages of *In Memoriam* – elicit any sympathy for the poet; mother-fixated or not, the poems of Browning show little desire to be mothered! There is no 'bardic persona' here between the reader and the poet, and the short staccato lines create an intimacy which seems more close than ordinary conversation. 'Where is the thread now? Off again!', the pauses give the sense of Browning groping for a conclusion which is almost within his reach and then melts away. They involve us in the poet's uncertainty which is the uncertainty of every man. The Tennysonian urgency of 'Just when I seemed about to learn!' is qualified by the ironic and resigned acceptance of 'The old trick!' The poem has an exceptional realization of the paradox of our destiny whereby knowledge may lead to ignorance and ignorance to knowledge. At the moment when we seem really to know, we are confronted with blank uncertainty. This is 'The old trick!' and it must be accepted. 'Off again!', such a casual ironic phrase – it refers to life in general and human life in particular – gives a resonance to the last two lines of the poem; a resonance which is neither comic nor tragic but a blend of these attitudes.

Although much of the greatest poetry is in a confessional form, the poet writing directly about some personal experience, it would have little interest if the poet's experience was not shared by a number of people. When one is moved by a poem then the author has, however obliquely, written one's autobiography. Confessional poetry is about other people as well as the poet and, conversely, poems about other people are about their author. Browning once excused himself to Elizabeth Barrett for not writing autobiographical poems; but although he may have shared the arbitrary assumption that the greatest poetry is directly confessional, it seems obvious enough that he is deeply involved with his dramatic monologues.

No doubt the satisfaction Browning found in expressing himself through other people of other ages is related to his ironic but passionate attitude towards his own experience. Henry James in *The Private Life* has written about the exceptional anonymity of Browning in his later age. The Baconian theory as to the authorship of Shakespeare's plays expresses a similar bafflement at an author who disappears from behind his own works. Sometimes the life of a writer – one thinks of Shelley and Byron, Oscar Wilde and, in our own time, Dylan Thomas and possibly Sylvia Plath – is among their most interesting works and, because of our unflagging appetite for gossip, one that has immediate appeal. Browning's creative life is for the most part submerged in his creations and it is hard to sweat out any neat autobiographical significance from Fra Lippo, Andrea del Sarto or the Dying Bishop. This may be frustrating to critics who hope to explain or explain away a writer's work by incidents of his biography. It does not detract from the merit of the poems. Henry James remarked on the hearty obviousness of Browning's table talk in later life and, since he could find no relationship between the subtle poetry and the platitudes of the dinner table, suggested that the poetry was written by an invisible doppelganger. Certainly, when Browning tries to reveal himself with 'simple directness' we often get just the obviousness remarked by James. When the poet does justice to his own experience then as in *Two in the Campagna* the result is extremely complex. For a comparatively simple but accurate statement of some aspect of his personal daemon we must read not such boisterous confessional pieces as *Prospice* or *Christmas-Eve*, but the monologues, poems in which he does express something of himself, at one remove.

In one of the greatest of these poems, *Childe Roland*,[1] it is obvious enough that Browning is the protagonist as he attempts to travel through a depression which cannot be avoided or wished away on to other people. The 'dark night of the soul' cannot be exorcized by a name but given some blink of the eye, some shift of vision and it can be seen.

> Not see? because of night perhaps? – Why, day
> Came back again for that! before it left,
> The dying sunset kindled through a cleft:

[1] I discuss the poem more fully in the section on Imagery, see below, p. 193 *ff*.

The hills, like giants at a hunting, lay —
Chin upon hand, to see the game at bay, —
'Now stab and end the creature — to the heft!'

As in *Two in the Campagna* we have an exact correspondence between the pauses and movements of language and the checks and movement of thought and feeling. There is also the embodiment of Browning's dread. He dwindles into a pygmy before the great predatory hills that look down on him.

In few of the monologues is there this closeness between Browning and his protagonist. But if the monologue is successful then one may assume that a marriage has occurred, that the poet has infused some element of himself into his creation, whether it is a bishop or a painter, an irascible monk or a Renaissance nobleman. The monologues fail when no particular conflict or problem of the essential Browning is involved and he writes merely from a sense of duty and his intelligence. Little else lies behind the impersonal sermonizing of *Rabbi Ben Ezra*. When Browning is involved in a monologue then its protagonist comes fully alive within a short poem. *My Last Duchess* encompasses a novel in about sixty lines, a sense of the infinite complexity of life, of the under and overtones of existence that is reminiscent of the work of D. H. Lawrence. One must set this poem, among many other masterpieces of technique, against the clumsy obviousness of his failures; failures of technique and sentiment which I have discussed in an earlier chapter. The Duke of this poem does not come alive by direct description. We are not told that 'there was a wart on the left nostril from which sprouted a long thick hair; and a certain slackness of the thin cruel mouth'. The essence of the Duke's personality is in the texture of the language. His frigid decorum is created by the imperceptible but unfailing rhyming couplets. His inhuman drawl is made alive through the feminine and often sibilant rhymes – 'munificence – pretence', 'commands – stands', 'thought a rarity – cast in bronze for me'. Browning evokes the Duke in a solitude which is peopled by his dead wife, his future wife and the emissary of his future father-in-law. His ability to suggest other people – the sons of the dying bishop, for instance, from the meditation of one person depends upon the extreme skill with which he tracks the moods and thoughts of his protagonist. Other people grow out of the developing moods not so much by description – the protagonist is too close to them for that – as incantation.

> Oh, Sir, she smiled, no doubt,
> Whene'er I passed her; but who passed without
> Much the same smile? This grew; I gave commands;
> Then all smiles stopped together.

The Duke's dead wife is conjured up before us like an apparition, or a figure in a vivid dream. The Bishop lies in St Praxed's Church in a limbo which reminds us of the state of William Golding's Pincher Martin. As he hovers between life and death, his sons appear and disappear with the sharpness of nightmare.

> All *lapis*, all, sons! Else I give the Pope
> My villas: will ye ever eat my heart?
> Ever your eyes were as a lizard's quick,
> They glitter like your mother's for my soul . . .

Beside the confessional poem and dramatic monologue, Browning wrote narrative verse. A good deal of it, though recorded in anthology after inbred anthology, is very indifferent work. But some of his best poems are in this form. *The Statue and the Bust* is an extremely well told story and its ending is clinched by a personal statement which, as is often the case with the best work of Browning, is both passionate and ironic. After describing the withering away of two destined lovers who lacked the courage to consummate their love he brings his story to heel in the present moment.

> And the sin I impute to each frustrate ghost
>
> Was, the unlit lamp and the ungirt loin,
> Though the end in sight was a crime, I say.
> You of the virtue, (we issue join)
> How strive you? *De te, fabula!*

Undoubtedly we do find some banal and didactic optimism in the bad verse of Browning. But here a moral affirmation is made with an irony and lightness of touch that should be sympathetic to our own age. The lightness is in the movement of the verse, the cynical bracketing of 'we issue join'; a phrase which both associates and dissociates the poet with the respectable people whose opinions he has flouted by suggesting that in certain circumstances adultery may be 'moral'. Moreover, *'De te, fabula!'* – whether we like it or not this is our story since we are all involved in the complex issues of life.

There is the same moral conviction and casualness in the ending of *Dîs Aliter Visum*. I have mentioned this account of an old but famous poet who has denied his affinity with a younger woman because of expediency. The last verse gives with extreme force the personal sterility which may result from a denial of impulse and the way this denial affects other people. The unspecified nature of the injury 'ankle or something' suggests the old poet's complete indifference to his mistress. 'Here comes my husband from his whist', the flat final line exactly catches the woman's bored resignation and the fact that she is trapped in an utterly meaningless routine.

> For Stephanie sprained last night her wrist,
>   Ankle or something. 'Pooh,' cry you?
> At any rate she danced, all say,
>   Vilely; her vogue has had its day.
> Here comes my husband from his whist.

The oddities of rhyme and rhythm which disfigure some of Browning's verse come in part from a kind of gymnastic exuberance, for he is one of the greatest masters of technique in English poetry. Indeed as regards metrical variety and innovation he is perhaps unequalled. It is hard to think of any other poet whose stylistic range is so great. There is a Shakespearean amplitude in a gift which includes the lyrical tenderness of *A Woman's Last Word*, the charged meditative blank verse of *Karshish* and *Cleon*, the rhapsodic *Invocation* to Elizabeth Barrett, the twilight monologue of *Andrea del Sarto* and the almost unbearable counterpointing of pity and savage jocularity in *The Heretic's Tragedy*.

One of Browning's finest poems and perhaps his most remarkable technical achievement is *A Toccata of Galuppi's*.[1] This work does not describe music, an effort almost certainly doomed to failure. Just as

[1] *Men and Women.*

Browning creates people by the movement of his verse rather than by description, so this poem gives some essence of Galuppi's clavichord[1] music by the subtle flow and pause of its rhythms. The ostensible theme of the poem is Venice at about the time of the Austrian occupation when the city had lost both the great art and industry of her past. She was the 'play city' of the world and her rich aristocracy had little occupation but a search for pleasure.

Did young people take their pleasure when the sea was
    warm in May?
Balls and masks begun at midnight, burning ever to mid-
    day,
When they made up fresh adventures for the morrow, do
    you say?

Browning senses in the music of Galuppi an elegiac lament for the mutability of physical beauty and pleasure. Though the poem and its music – the two are indistinguishable – comment on the moth-like evanescence of pleasure, they do so with a grave compassion which is not unlike the dirge from *Cymbeline*:

Golden lads and girls all must,
As chimney-sweepers, come to dust.[2]

With extraordinary skill the poem catches up into the modulations of the clavichord rhythms the breathless urgency – something between a sigh and articulate speech – of erotic communion. But the last line of this verse gives both a strong tragic undercurrent to the surface gaiety of the music and a sense of the physical

[1] In fact Galuppi composed mainly for the harpsichord.
[2] Shakespeare, *Cymbeline*, IV, ii.

177

decrepitude and death which underlie casual sensuality.

'Were you happy?' – 'Yes.' – 'And are you still as
    happy?' – 'Yes – And you?'
– 'Then more kisses' – 'Did *I* stop them, when a million
    seemed so few?'
Hark – the dominant's persistence, till it must be answered
    to!

The faltering uncertainty of the 'lovers' is communicated by the movement of the verse, by the gasp (it is an unacknowledged caesura!) that is suggested by the break in the lines between 'as' and 'happy'.

Unlike Tennyson, Browning seems not uncertain of the immortality of the soul. Indeed his conviction is strong enough to be expressed with a humorous irony –

The soul, doubtless, is immortal – where a soul can be
    discerned.

The ironic suggestiveness of that remark depends upon the position of the word 'doubtless' and the break after 'immortal'. Browning gives to his verse the exact modulation of timing and tone which point the tale of a skilled conversationalist.

Like Lawrence he thinks of 'making the soul' of building a 'Ship of Death' which is capable of weathering eternity.

Butterflies may dread extinction, – you'll not die, it cannot
    be!

Galuppi's strenuous existence has fitted him for immortality, but Browning's elegy ends, as is so often the case with this poet, on a question. What is the fate of

men and women who have lived solely by temporal
values and seem to bear no relevance to death?

'As for Venice and its people, merely born to bloom and
drop,
Here on earth they bore their fruitage, mirth and folly were
the crop.
What of soul was left, I wonder, when the kissing had to
stop?

'Dust and ashes!' So you creak it, and I want the heart to
scold.
Dear dead women, with such hair, too – what's become of
all the gold
Used to hang and brush their bosoms? I feel chilly and
grown old.

The last two verses gather power as the toccata draws
to its climax. The grandeur of the end is created by the
language, by the alliterative vowels of 'born to bloom',
by the richness of 'bore their fruitage'. But in the last
two lines Browning brings the poem back to that
intimate and compassionate questioning which is an
especial quality of his work. 'With such hair, too' – the
aside is both ironical and tender. The dead women
come alive again as Browning questions their fate.
Finally, in the last short statement – 'I feel chilly and
grown old' – he creates an intimacy between himself
and the reader which binds his poem to a tense which
is always present.

II

The images of Browning's poetry break away from the
vision of Nature which is characteristic of much of the

work of the Romantics and, in a modified form, of his great contemporary, Tennyson. His work, far more than that of Gerard Manley Hopkins, is the beginning of the poetry of our own age. The stark often terrifying images of such a poem as *Childe Roland* anticipate the rats, bones and squalid canals of T. S. Eliot's *Waste Land*. Browning enlarges the field of poetic experience and to express his new themes and explorations he draws his images from phenomena which if not new to poetry had been left almost untouched since the 17th century.

As Matthew Arnold points out in his *Memorial Verses to Wordsworth*, poets do restore to us through the open vision of their work a vivid apprehension of the natural world; an apprehension which we tend to lose as we grow older and crust over reality with certain platitudes of thought and vision. But the Romantics tended to concentrate on particular phenomena of Nature and a particular way of seeing these phenomena. They wrote about winds, mountains, the moon, turbulent streams, birds, caverns and fountains because through them they could body forth those areas of human and inhuman experience which were their especial theme.

Of course they did not consider these phenomena merely as images. Shelley's *Ode to the West Wind* celebrates not only the zest and urgency of life but an actual wind disturbing the trees and sea over which it passes. The visionary passages of *The Prelude* are always initiated by some physical experience. For Wordsworth the natural and supernatural world are intimately related. The crags of the Lake District make him aware of 'unknown modes of being' because he has clambered over their rock and turf.

180

> I have hung
> Above the raven's nest, by knots of grass
> And half-inch fissures in the slippery rock
> But ill sustained, and almost (so it seemed)
> Suspended by the blast that blew amain,
> Shouldering the naked crag . . .

It is always a double vision. Nature provides poets with counterparts and resemblances with which to embody some psychological or spiritual insight. She is also known as herself, and with that intimacy which is a condition of knowledge.

The Romantic poets knew certain aspects of Nature. Neither Wordsworth, Coleridge, Shelley nor Keats exhausted her infinite variety. But readers and critics of poetry have tended to generalize the vision of these men, and imagine that it alone constitutes a truly 'poetic' appreciation of man and his environment. It is this generalization that lies behind the astonishing condemnation of Browning by Edith Batho and Bonamy Dobrée in their book *The Victorians and After*.[1] 'There is little sensuous in his verse, perhaps not a line that one repeats as one does Tennyson's

> The moan of doves in immemorial elms
> The murmur of innumerable bees . . .

The Romantic interpretation of Nature which should have given us 'a way of looking' tended to become '*the* way of looking'. But experience which does not progress must regress – there is no standing still. The dead end of the attempt to stabilize a poetic vision were the bluebell woods and 'lovesome' gardens of the weaker Georgians.

The illumination of today may become the platitude

[1] *The Victorians and After, 1830–1914* (Cresset, 1951).

of the day after tomorrow. Tennyson is perhaps the last great poet whose vision of Nature, though intimate and personal, resembles that of the great Romantics. But despite the resemblance, Tennyson pays that close attention to the intricate details of Nature which is characteristic of much Victorian poetry and our own age. Wordsworth was familiar with the Pleiades, but he would never have seen them as 'tangled in a silver braid'! Wordsworth often gives us images which show the close observation of the countryman – the spray of dew thrown up by a running hare, the crocus *snapped* by frost, the ice *yelling* as frost grips a lake. But such images are incidental to his main intention which has to do with the great sweeps of landscape and washes of cloud rather than intricate details.

There is a shift of sensibility. Tennyson with his closer view humanizes Nature and makes it correspond by his extremely selective vision with that nostalgia and rhapsodic anxiety which was the most constant atmosphere of his poetry. Wordsworth on the other hand was concerned with the impersonal energies which overshadow human nature, with that eternal 'selfness' of man to which temporary personality may be only an incident. To express his vision he not only concentrates on those aspects of Nature which are least domestic, but dehumanizes or rather depersonalizes people so as to associate them with those 'unknown modes of being' which were his particular theme. One thinks of the shepherd of *The Prelude* transfigured by the atmosphere of the mountains into an 'aerial cross' while his sheep loom through the mist like 'Greenland bears'. Or the Leech Gatherer of *Resolution and Independence* –

As a huge Stone is sometimes seen to lie
Couched on the bald top of an eminence;
Wonder to all who do the same espy,
By what means it could thither come, and whence;
So that it seems a thing endued with sense:
Like a Sea-beast crawled forth, that on a shelf
Of rock or sand reposeth, there to sun itself;
Such seemed this Man . . .[1]

Human beings do have this Wordsworthian impersonality. Indeed certain lives of especial serenity suggest that the nearer we approach psychological wholeness the more impersonal we become and, paradoxically, the more human. But there is also immediate personality, the finite ego, menaced by time and subjective conflict. In the greatest poetry of the Romantics, there is seldom a keen apprehension of such complicated, everyday and anxious humanity. The protagonists of the *Thorn* and *The Idiot Boy* are drawn with a sparse simplicity. It is true that in many passages of *The Prelude* Wordsworth writes about himself, but his chief concern is not with the intimate details of relationship and daily life, but those moments when man transcends his complex humanity. In his fine 'secondary' poetry, *Dejection,* for instance, or *Frost at Midnight,* Coleridge treats of human problems; but not with a power and insight that can compare with the human being as archetype, as in *The Ancient Mariner* or *Kubla Khan.* Nor is Shelley concerned with the intricacies of psychological motivation and conflict – at least as it takes place in the immediate arena of personality. His interest lay in that metaphysical dimension

---

[1] Wordsworth, *The Leech Gatherer; or, Resolution and Independence.*

where the expression of personality and certain great patterns of thought are indistinguishable. Prometheus is an archetypal idea rather than a man. Wordsworth did know both worlds, the human and superhuman, natural and supernatural. But in his 'great period' he is so thoroughly at home in both of them as to appear – since most of us do not breathe very easily in the timeless world – a trifle inhuman.

Tennyson and Browning are usually concerned with personal problems and conflict. It is true that both poets write about mystical experience where man expands beyond his ordinary personality and the limitations of time and space. But it is unlikely that they had such sustained mystical insight, as Blake or Wordsworth. Certainly Browning's finest poetry is concerned with the tensions, speculations and achievements of a human psyche which, though it has a timeless significance, is for the moment involved in time and space and a serviceable body.

In the work of Tennyson there is the same concern with immediate personality. But his work, for all its great merit, tends to be self-enclosed. He is rarely able to use either his unease or self-knowledge – as Browning does in poem after poem – as a way of exploring the predicament of other people. Consequently though one is deeply moved by Tennyson's poetry it may be with a certain reservation. Often his intention seems not so much to gain insight and resolution as the reader's sympathy. This applies to many fine passages of *In Memoriam* and such a lyric as

> Break, break, break,
> On thy cold grey stones, O Sea!

One thinks of the widow who casting herself in a paroxysm of grief before Pope John XXIII was told, 'Madam, this is not the true life', and realizes that poetry can have a more serious intention.

Browning has a more serious intention. But the poets share at least one quality which distinguishes them from the Romantics. Their main concern is not, as in Coleridge's *Ancient Mariner*, with man as archetype. Unlike Shelley with his Prometheus and Alastor they do not write about man as the personification of an idea. Nor – one thinks of Wordsworth and his vagrants, forsaken women, shepherds and holy fools – have they much interest in the human being sweated down to some pristine simplicity. They write of men – for Tennyson it is usually himself – as a finite and divided creature. He moves, it is true, on the edge of 'worlds not realized' but he retains his complex humanity. To express their own aspirations and the closely observed men and women of their poetry Tennyson and Browning draw on the 'infinite particularities' of Nature rather than the vast shapes of her mountains or the unparagraphed energy of sea and wind. Thus the depression and self-imprisonment of Tennyson's *Mariana* is communicated by the almost obsessive details. They suggest that she has turned against her own vitality and become a thing among the drift of things.

> The sparrow's chirrup on the roof,
>   The slow clock ticking, and the sound
> Which to the wooing wind aloof
>   The poplar made, did all confound
> Her sense; but most she loathed the hour
>   When the thick-moted sunbeam lay

185

Athwart the chambers, and the day
Was sloping toward his western bower.
Then, said she, 'I am very dreary,
He will not come,' she said;
She wept, 'I am aweary, aweary,
Oh God, that I were dead!'

When Browning wishes to communicate the state of
mind of the Bishop of St Praxed who though dying is
still rooting among material values and desire, he does
so by natural description whose precisely observed
details have a sensuousness that is over-ripe, gross.

My sons, ye would not be my death? Go dig
The white-grape vineyard where the oil-press stood,
Drop water gently till the surface sinks,
And if ye find . . . Ah, God I know not, I! . . .
Bedded in store of rotten figleaves soft,
And corded up in a tight olive-frail,
Some lump, ah God, of *lapis lazuli*,
Big as a Jew's head cut off at the nape,
Blue as a vein o'er the Madonna's breast . . .

Although like all poets both the Romantics and Victorians are concerned with the psyche, with an interpretation of the inner life of man, the Victorians are
far more concerned with the 'ego' than the 'self'. I
mean that whereas Wordsworth, Coleridge – in his
three greatest poems – Shelley and Keats, usually write
about those periods of insight, intense grief and aspiration where a man or woman seem to transcend their
everyday humanity, Tennyson and Browning write for
the most part about the aspirations and problems of
everyday people.

To say this is not to belittle the achievement of these

poets. Indeed insight into such immediate problems may be a particular task of our age. But the point is that the shift of interest from the impersonal and infinite significance of man to his personal and finite significance is reflected in the much more detailed view which the Victorians take of Nature.

Tennyson's observation is close and selective, and he selects for the most part in order to create a sense of nostalgia and anxiety, of the finite human being menaced by time and the impersonal ever-changing forces of Nature.

> Tonight the winds begin to rise
> And roar from yonder dropping day:
> The last red leaf is whirl'd away,
> The rooks are blown about the skies;
>
> The forest crack'd, the waters curl'd,
> The cattle huddled on the lea;
> And wildly dash'd on tower and tree
> The sunbeam strikes along the world . . .[1]

Browning looks at Nature with an interest which resembles that of the zoologist and botanist. What fascinates him and determines his imagery is the spawning vitality of the animal and vegetable world, as in this passage from *Caliban upon Setebos*:

> Yon otter, sleek-wet, black, lithe as a leech;
> Yon auk, one fire-eye in a ball of foam,
> That floats and feeds; a certain badger brown
> He hath watched hunt with that slant white-wedge eye
> By moonlight; and the pie with the long tongue
> That pricks deep into oakwarts for a worm,
> And says a plain word when she finds her prize,

[1] *In Memoriam.*

But will not eat the ants; the ants themselves
That build a wall of seeds and settled stalks
About their hole –.

'You speak out, you,' Browning wrote to Elizabeth Barrett in 1845, 'I only make men and women speak, give you truth broken into prismatic hues, and fear the pure white light, even if it is in me, but I am going to try.' But despite this statement the poet does infuse himself into all his significant work. Wordsworth's *The Prelude* or Tennyson's *In Memoriam* would not be illuminating poems if their exploration of one man was not searching and honest enough to become – because of the common ground of our humanity – an examination of many other men and women. Conversely, if Browning's poems about other men and women were not at one and the same time about himself, if a kind of union had not taken place between himself and the men and women he writes about so that they are both themselves and indirect expressions of some aspect of Browning's personality, then the poems would lack vitality and general interest. Some essential quality of the poet is apparent in all his work. *Caliban*, for example, presents through images that have a zoological and botanical exactness the teeming fecundity of nature. The poem shows Browning's almost animalic relish ('what God hath created that call thou not common or unclean') of the infinite stimuli to which the senses are exposed.

Look now, I melt a gourd-fruit into mash,
Add honeycomb and pods, I have perceived,
Which bite like finches when they bill and kiss, –
Then, when froth rises bladdery, drink up all,
Quick, quick, till maggots scamper through my brain . . .

Browning gives substance and a spatial reality to the thought of his poems by tracking, as in *Two in the Campagna*, the movement of his thought with a cinematic observation of nature. Or he will intersperse, as in *By the Fire-side*, meditative passages with a photographic close-up which makes them alive in a particular moment and place.

Those early November hours –

> That crimson the creeper's leaf across
> Like a splash of blood, intense, abrupt,
> O'er a shield, else gold from rim to boss,
> And lay it for show on the fairy-cupped
> Elf-needled mat of moss,
>
> By the rose-flesh mushrooms, undivulged
> Last evening – nay, in to-day's first dew
> Yon sudden coral nipple bulged
> Where a freaked, fawn-coloured, flaky crew
> Of toad-stools peep indulged.

He gives the same fascinated and exact scrutiny to the world of men and women. It is not a question of man as spirit or animal, since both are manifestations of a single energy. Browning expresses both this belief and his delight in the paradoxical diversity of human nature through the early Renaissance monk and painter Fra Lippo Lippi.[1] Lippo Lippi has adopted the monastic life not through spiritual vocation but the necessity of avoiding starvation when a deserted orphan:

> I was a baby when my mother died
> And father died and left me in the street.
> I starved there, God knows how, a year or two

[1] *Men and Women.*

> On fig-skins, melon-parings, rinds and shucks,
> Refuse and rubbish.

It was while begging in Florence that the painter first
steeped himself in the life of the streets which he was
to express in his pictures. One notes in that passage
Browning's interest in the waif's food. 'Rinds and
shucks' suggest both the boy's intense will to live and
the poet's desire to find the exact words for the refuse
which sustained him.

Fra Lippo Lippi's monologue is spoken in a narrow
street where he has been accosted late at night by the
watch after a gay night 'on the town'.

> And I've been three weeks shut within my mew,
> A-painting for the great man, saints and saints
> And saints again. I could not paint all night –
> Ouf! I leaned out of window for fresh air.
> Then came a hurry of feet and little feet,
> A sweep of lute-strings, laughs, and whifts of song, –
>
> . . . .
>
> Scarce had they turned the corner when a titter,
> Like the skipping of rabbits by moonlight, – three slim
>   shapes –
> And a face that looked up .. . . zooks, sir, flesh and blood,
> That's all I'm made of! Into shreds it went,
> Curtain and counterpane and coverlet,
> All the bed furniture – a dozen knots,
> There was a ladder! down I let myself,
> Hands and feet, scrambling somehow, and so dropped,
> And after them.

Lippo is both an extremely individual human being
and a type. The painter represents the breakaway of
Renaissance art from symbols which are mainly devo-

tional to a celebration of the glory and spiritual significance of the world, of people of flesh and blood and every variety of mood and interest. Through Lippo Lippi Browning makes his most interesting examination of pictorial art, but the poet also expresses, one suspects, much of his own personality and creative zest through the painter. Here Lippo Lippi describes his first work on the walls of his monastery:

> . . . my head being crammed, their walls a blank,
> Never was such prompt disemburdening.
> First, every sort of monk, the black and white,
> I drew them, fat and lean: then, folks at church,
> From good old gossips waiting to confess
> Their cribs of barrel-droppings, candle-ends, —
> To the breathless fellow at the altar-foot,
> Fresh from his murder, safe and sitting there
> With the little children round him in a row
> Of admiration, half for his beard and half
> For that white anger of his victim's son
> Shaking a fist at him with one fierce arm,
> Signing himself with the other because of Christ
> (Whose sad face on the cross sees only this
> After the passion of a thousand years)
> Till some poor girl, her apron o'er her head
> Which the intense eyes looked through, came at eve
> On tip-toe, said a word, dropped in a loaf,
> Her pair of ear-rings and a bunch of flowers
> The brute took growling, prayed, and then was gone.

That passage shows Browning's concern, not only with the diversity of life but its dramatic, almost unresolvable contrasts and conflict. We have the little children admiring the murderer, the bereaved son crossing himself while white with hatred, the intense girl still in love with the 'brute' who is incapable of affection.

191

Just as experience of the outer world makes us aware of ourselves, so it is self-knowledge which enables us to know other people. And it is those problems which are best understood and most deeply felt within ourselves which we can divine and interpret in others. It may have been Browning's capacity for fixation which enabled him to create Andrea del Sarto and the Duke of *My Last Duchess*. Certainly his zest for life and acute sensory awareness are responsible for the spawning vitality of his nature images. He was also more aware of evil, of the shadow side of human nature than any poet of his age.

No doubt he knew evil because he had experienced it within himself; he certainly knew the sterility and self-destructiveness of acute depression.

'For every poor speck of a Vesuvius or a Stromboli in my microcosm', he wrote to Elizabeth Barrett, 'there are huge layers of ice and pits of black cold water – and I make the most of my two or three fire eyes, because I know by experience, alas, how these tend to extinction – and the ice grows and grows – still this last is true part of me, most characteristic part, best part, perhaps, and I disown nothing – only when you talked of knowing me!'

The need to body out the sense of inner darkness and depression which that letter expresses, to find poetic equivalents for the destructiveness he divined in himself and the world about him is responsible for Browning's most dramatic expansion of the field of poetic imagery. Perhaps the need to encounter the shadow side of the psyche is particularly acute in our own age and not unconnected with the deaths of such writers as Dylan Thomas and Ernest Heming-

way. To express the violence and duplicity of men and
women and the way our lives may shade off into
nightmare, Browning drew on the distortion and sick-
ness of Nature, broken and tortured animals, sinister
machines. In doing this he is the initiator of much of
the poetry of our own age, poetry which uses similar
images to explore the same darkness.

In *Childe Roland*[1] we find his most startling use of
landscape to create a sense of the mystery and laby-
rinthine complexity of the human psyche and the
strange, often savage fauna which inhabit it. The poem
describes a man's journey into the interior darkness of
himself in order to confront that nexus of destructive
energy which Jungians call the Shadow. It is the same
journey that Theseus takes when, holding on to reality
by the slender thread of Ariadne, he descends into the
Cretan Maze and battles with the Minotaur. Theseus
actually encounters the Shadow which is endowed by
the myth with the shape of a bull man – that is to say,
human nature dominated by the animalic forces of the
Unconscious. An antagonist is valid enough since dis-
sociated energy does appear to have independent existence – hence the identification in the Gospels of lunacy
with demonic possession.

Browning's poem, however, ends at the moment before encounter, the moment Roland blows the slug-
horn to summon the demon from the tower.

> There they stood, ranged along the hill-sides – met
> To view the last of me, a living frame
> For one more picture! in a sheet of flame
> I saw them and I knew them all. And yet

---

[1] '*Childe Roland to the Dark Tower Came*' (*Men and Women*).

Dauntless the slug-horn to my lips I set
And blew. '*Childe Roland to the Dark Tower came.*'

The absence of a personified antagonist does not make Childe Roland's ordeal any less valid. The journey is itself the ordeal. The encounter is not as with Theseus, a wrestling with the Minotaur at the centre of the Maze, but the overcoming of the horror and dread of the journey to the Tower. One thinks of Conrad's story, *The Heart of Darkness*.[1] On one level it tells of an actual journey its author made up the Congo, on another of just such a penetration into the darkness of the psyche. Conrad's mouthpiece, Marlowe, is going to meet a trader called Kurtz. Kurtz is a real ivory trader who has played on the superstition of the natives to gain divine, or rather demonic power over them. He is also a personification of the Shadow and as such he must be a shadowy though awe-inspiring figure.

'He rose, unsteady, long, pale, indistinct, like a vapour exhaled by the earth, and swayed slightly, misty and silent before me; while at my back the fires loomed from the trees, and the murmur of many voices issued from the forest.'

Kurtz is a figure of suggestiveness and power but he is only a part of Marlowe's ordeal. At least as important is the voyage in the rickety little steamer, the negotiating of snags, the lunatic jabbering and despairing cries from the jungle, the drums, the flight of spears from a curtain of foliage. This also is the ordeal.

Browning's poem dispenses with any personified antagonist and concentrates on the journey. There is no need for an antagonist because the poet makes the

[1] Dent (1946).

terrain which Childe Roland crosses so sinister and
infernal that any final antagonist would be an anti-
climax.

> Now blotches rankling, coloured gay and grim,
>   Now patches where some leanness of the soil's
>   Broke into moss or substances like boils;
> Then came some palsied oak, a cleft in him
> Like a distorted mouth that splits its rim
>   Gaping at death, and dies while it recoils.

This is the horror the knight has to wrestle with and
the fact that he does go steadily on through his nightmare landscape means that by the time he reaches the
Tower he has succeeded in his ordeal.

As in all the myths and significant dreams to which
this poem is related, once its hero has embarked on his
quest there is no possibility of return. One cannot return to a comfortable if superficial existence once the
journey of exploration into the recesses of the self has
been started.

> For mark! no sooner was I fairly found
>   Pledged to the plain, after a pace or two,
>   Than pausing to throw backward a last view
> To the safe road, 'twas gone! grey plain all round!
> Nothing but plain to the horizon's bound.
>   I might go on; nought else remained to do.

The journey is akin to the 'dark night of the soul'.
Childe Roland tries to ward off the despair and depression it entails by thinking of the 'good old days',
but one by one his defences are stripped away from him
and proved useless till all that is left is himself and the
dark path he has to travel.

I shut my eyes and turned them on my heart.
　As a man calls for wine before he fights,
　I asked one draught of earlier, happier sights
Ere fitly I could hope to play my part.
Think first, fight afterwards – the soldier's art:
　One taste of the old times sets all to rights!

Giles, then, the soul of honour – there he stands
　Frank as ten years ago when knighted first.
　What honest men should dare (he said) he durst.
Good – but the scene shifts – faugh! what hangman's
　　hands
Pin to his breast a parchment? his own bands
　Read it. Poor traitor, spit upon and curst!

Roland is facing the negative, destructive energies
of himself on his journey, so the wilderness shows signs
of furious conflict. But it is a war within the psyche
that Browning is concerned with in this poem; its in-
wardness is brought home by the fact that the battle
has always just taken place and the combatants are
never present.

　　Who were the strugglers, what war did they wage
　Whose savage trample thus could pad the dank
　Soil to a plash? toads in a poisoned tank,
　　Or wild cats in a red-hot iron cage . . .

The sense of inward corruption which mystics and
psychologists tell us must accompany the 'dark night
of the soul' is suggested by the diseased landscape.

As for the grass, it grew as scant as hair
　In leprosy – thin dry blades pricked the mud
　Which underneath looked kneaded up with blood.

The Unconscious may be the source of creative inspiration and a wisdom and benevolence which exceeds

individual personality, but it is also the matrix of homicidal violence and such destructive energy as was once symbolized by the were-wolf and the vampire. The poem describes an encounter with those destructive powers, and one of its achievements lies in having made the nightmare articulate and observable in the light of day, while maintaining a spectral resonance. The fact that the wilderness reeks with evil, but one never meets the cause of this evil, whether human or inhuman, means that it is not wished away on to someone or something 'out there', but is a quality of a human being, of that Everyman who is Childe Roland.

> And more than that – a furlong on – why, there!
>> What bad use was that engine for, that wheel,
>> Or brake, not wheel – that harrow fit to reel
> Men's bodies out like silk? with all the air
> Of Tophet's tool, on earth left unaware,
>> Or brought to sharpen its rusty teeth of steel.

For a counterpart to that infernal machine, indeed to almost any of the terrifying images of the poem, one must go back to the Jacobeans, to the Cardinal of the *Duchess of Malfi*, for instance, who says in his mania:

> When I walk by the fishponds in my garden
> I seem to see a thing armed with a rake
> That strikes at me.

But Browning's image is sharper and more fully realized than Webster's because in Browning the savagery of the unconscious has shouldered up nearer to conscious awareness than with the Jacobean dramatist. For all its ghostly suggestiveness the poem is near

197

to insight and conscious thought. It is this which gives it the sense of a dream of which one almost but not quite possesses the meaning.

No doubt it is this insight into evil and the vitality with which it is expressed which has led earlier critics who were well-disposed to Browning's optimistic banalities to ignore the darker side of his work. Hostile contemporary critics, one thinks of John Heath-Stubbs in *The Darkling Plain*, have also belittled this exploration of the poet: it is bad or 'unhealthy' taste. But it is the contention of this writer that good taste does not consist in ignoring the satanic element of man which whether accepted or not will insist on a hearing.

Childe Roland treats of negative energy as it operates within the arena of a single human psyche. In most of Browning's dark poems we see it projected outwards into action and affecting the external world. *My Last Duchess* and *The Ring and the Book* are an examination of evil within the sphere of personal relationship. In two poems, *Holy-Cross Day* and a masterpiece, *The Heretic's Tragedy*, Browning is concerned with evil as a collective or group phenomenon. *Holy-Cross Day*[1] tells of that form of mediaeval persecution by which the Jews were forced to attend a Christian service and pretend that they had been converted to Christianity. A Jew is the protagonist of the poem and in its first section comments on the service with a humour which though savage and ribald does not disguise the poet's deep pity.

> Fee, faw, fum! bubble and squeak!
> Blessedest Thursday's the fat of the week.

[1] *Dramatic Lyrics and Romances.*

Rumble and tumble, sleek and rough,
Stinking and savoury, smug and gruff,
Take the church-road, for the bell's due chime
Gives us the summons – 'tis sermon-time!

Groan altogether now, whee-hee-hee!
It's a-work, it's a-work, ah, woe is me!
It began, when a herd of us, picked and placed,
Were spurred through the Corso, stripped to
        the waist;
Jew brutes, with sweat and blood well spent
To usher in worthily Christian Lent.

In the second part of the poem, Rabbi Ben Ezra's Song
of Death, the savage humour gives way to Browning's
compassion

By the torture, prolonged from age to age,
By the infamy, Israel's heritage,
By the Ghetto's plague, by the garb's dis-
        grace,
By the badge of shame, by the felon's
        place,
By the branding tool, the bloody whip,
And the summons to Christian fellowship, –

We boast our proof that at least the Jew
Would wrest Christ's name from the Devil's
        crew.

The urgency of this poem and Browning's use of the
term 'Jew brutes' are significant. Although he lived in
an age when it was customary to slur over the reality
of personal and social evil and believe that civilization
had almost tamed human ferocity it is only in his
superficial work that he shares this facile optimism. In

199

at least two of his poems, *The Ring and the Book* and *The Heretic's Tragedy*,[1] he shows an understanding both of the purely destructive energy which is latent in human nature, and man's capacity to work out paranoid delusions on a gigantic social scale which, until these realities were banged home to us by the Hitler régime was equalled by few writers. For an age which does not have many illusions about human perfectibility, the fact that Browning expressed himself through a domestic crime in 17th-century Italy and the destruction of the Knights Templar by the Inquisition in the 14th century will not affect the reality of his premonition.

The Knights Templar were founded at the beginning of the 12th century and their object was to guard pilgrims to the Holy Land. They combined the mediaeval ideals of monk and knight and by 1260 numbered 20,000 including many rich and powerful aristocrats. They owned the islands of Cyprus and Malta and their great wealth, power and independence aroused the jealousy both of the Church and State. In 1305 Philip the Fair of France, acting through his puppet, Pope Clement V, enticed the Grand Master of the Templars, Jacques de Molay (Browning calls him John of the Temple in his poem), from Cyprus to Paris. Many other Templars, including both the leaders of the order and its rank and file, joined the Grand Master. Then, when Philip had called in his city the bulk of the order the pogrom began. It was conducted through the Inquisition and, after torture, most of the Templars confessed to various trumped up

[1] *The Heretic's Tragedy; a middle-Age Interlude* (*Dramatic Lyrics and Romances*).

charges, including heresy. Before their death both Jacques de Molay and Gaufrid de Charney, his second-in-command, declared their innocence and as an extra punishment were roasted alive over a slow fire. Jacques de Molay is supposed to have summoned both king and pope to meet him at the bar of God within a year; both died within that period.

The burning of Molay summoned all Browning's creative power, and *The Heretic's Tragedy*, though never anthologized, is one of his greatest poems. The terror of the theme, the compassion for the Grand Master and the sympathy for his broad but heretical belief 'That God is good and the rest is breath', are treated with an ironic gaiety which brings home to us, far more sharply than solemn declamation and disapproval, both the state of mind of Molay's persecutors and the horror of his death, not only as a real event but one relevant to every moment of existence. There is an almost Gilbertian swing about the poem's brisk rhythms and the obviousness of its rhymes. This is quite deliberate and communicates the self-righteous smugness of John's tormentors, the self-enclosed thought and feeling behind their mercenary *auto-da-fé*.

> In the midst is a goodly gallows built;
>   'Twixt fork and fork, a stake is stuck;
> But first they set divers tumbrils a-tilt,
>   Make a trench all round with the city muck;
> Inside they pile log upon log, good store;
>   Faggots no few, blocks great and small,
> Reach a man's mid-thigh, no less, no more, –
>   For they mean he should roast in the sight
>   of all.

CHORUS
We mean he should roast in the sight of all.

Good sappy bavins that kindle forthwith;
 Billets that blaze substantial and slow;
Pine-stump split deftly, dry as pith;
 Larch-heart that chars to a chalk-white glow:
Then up they hoist me John in a chafe,
 Sling him fast like a hog to scorch,
Spit in his face, then leap back safe,
 Sing 'Laudes' and bid clap-to the torch.

CHORUS
Laus Deo – who bids clap-to the torch.

The jaunty rhythm clashes with the horrible event
which those verses hammer home by an accumulation
of detail. They create in the mind a tension between
the wish to feel the world is a harmless enough place
and its inhabitants fairly benevolent, and the in-
escapable fact that there are destructive forces abroad
which make such security quite untenable. 'We mean
he should roast in the sight of all', 'We bring John now
to be burned alive', such single lines of 'Chorus' make
it impossible to wish away the crime on to some institution or impersonal energy. This, it underlines, is
the responsibility of individual people not very different from ourselves. Yet the italicized lines of the
chorus do link the event with the Church and so suggest that the human psyche can pervert a religion of
charity and wisdom to its own savage and fanatical intentions. Thus the poem's climax of brutality, a verse
which describes John's total subjection to his persecutors so that his humanity is reduced to mere material

for their intention, which is the infliction of pain, is associated with the sign of the Cross.

> John of the Temple, whose fame so bragged,
>   Is burning alive in Paris square!
> How can he curse, if his mouth is gagged?
>   Or wriggle his neck, with a collar there?
> Or heave his chest, which a band goes round?
>   Or threat with his fist, since his arms are
>   spliced?
> Or kick with his feet, now his legs are bound?
>   – Thinks John, I will call upon Jesus Christ.
>   *[Here one crosseth himself.*

The Templars were associated with some heretical and mystical doctrine which may have anticipated the Rosicrucian mystery of the 16th century in that it combined in one symbol the Cross of creative suffering and the Rose of love. Browning uses this image of the rose with tremendous power. First in the mystical sense. John of the Temple

> – Saith he knoweth but one thing, – what he
>   knows?
> That God is good and the rest is breath;
> Why else is the same styled Sharon's rose?
> Once a rose, ever a rose, he saith.

> CHORUS

> O, John shall yet find a rose, he saith!

Then it is the rose of sensuality; and since Browning does not idealize the Templars and so make them unreal and sentimental there is a hint here of the homosexual practices of which they were accused by the Inquisition.

> Alack, there be roses and roses, John!
>   Some, honied of taste like your leman's
>   tongue . . .

Finally the rose becomes the fire and smoke in which John is enveloped.

> Ha ha, John plucketh now at his rose
>   To rid himself of a sorrow at heart!
> Lo, – petal on petal, fierce rays unclose;
>   Anther on anther, sharp spikes outstart;
> And with blood for dew, the bosom boils;
>   And a gust of sulphur is all its smell;
> And lo, he is horribly in the toils
>   Of a coal-black giant flower of hell!

> CHORUS
> What maketh heaven, That maketh hell.

Flame, rose and scorching flesh are all gathered up by the beauty and terror of the image. The flat statement of the Chorus as to the ambivalence of creation ('Did He who made the lamb, make thee'?) is given enormous power by its prosaic flatness. Finally we have the crescendo of John's death.

> And his voice, like a mad dog's choking bark,
> At the steady whole of the Judge's face –
> Died. Forth John's soul flared into the dark.

It is followed by one line of great quiet which sums up Browning's attitude to the terrible event he has re-created in his poem.

> God help all poor souls lost in the dark!

Since the poet knew a great deal about evil, he understood its inevitable relation with ignorance and lack of insight, that, in fact, 'they know not what they do'

Chapter Six

Conclusion

Well, British Public, ye who like me not,
(God love you!) and will have your proper laugh
At the dark question, laugh it! I laugh first.
            The Ring and the Book (Bk I).

The dark question which Browning asks in poem after
poem must remain unanswered. It is concerned with
the relevance of thought, feeling, action, indeed of all
finite experience to eternity. Though it is possible that
'Eternity is in love with the productions of time', we
who are children of time can have no definitive knowledge of Eternity. At least until we have been born
into it through death. In the great tradition which
stretches through Plato and Blake, Yeats and D. H.
Lawrence, Browning, although not a mystic, believes
that out of the fragments of everyday behaviour we
must build our ship of death, create within mortality
some spiritual essence that is fitted for immortality.
That dimension may have no more reality to a living
man or woman than this present world may have to
an unborn child. But the endless speculation of
mystics, poets and philosophers about the destiny of
the soul suggests that our personal development is not
circumscribed by personality and is towards an order

205

of being where such terms as time and space are without meaning.

In his greatest poems, while keeping close to the complex conflicting experience of men and women, Browning shows how this experience slides off and 'onward whenever light winds blow' from what can be apprehended by sense and known by the intellect. 'Being' exceeds any definition and the questions we ask as to the ultimate nature and intention of Being cannot be answered. What matters is the pertinence of the questioning and the effort which goes into creating this pertinence is as near as we can come to an answer. Few poets ask such significant and strenuous questions as Robert Browning. Much of his best work strives towards a knowledge of 'ultimate issues' which must always be out of reach. It creates a strenuous uncertainty which may lie at the end of enquiry; an uncertainty which for this age may be a form of faith.

Index

207

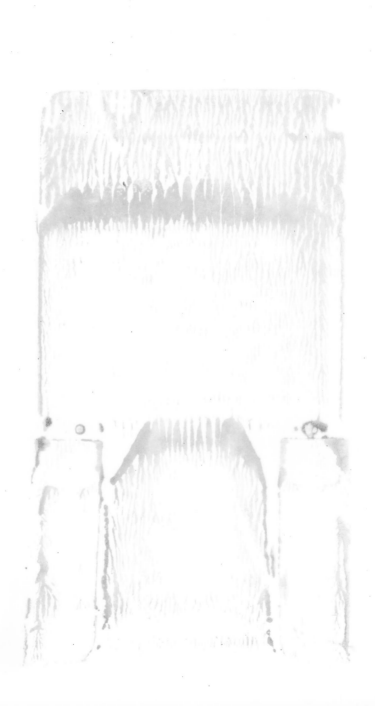